AACR 2

an introduction to the
second edition of
Anglo-American Cataloguing Rules

ERRATA AND ADDITIONAL COMMENTS

Despite the great care taken in the writing and production of this book, the author regrets that, unfortunately, a few errors remained undetected until after the work had gone to press.

General   A space should be interposed consistently between the number and the abbreviation p. in the pagination of a printed monography, eg 273 p.

Frames 9 and 11   Three spaces are required before the specific material designation v. in the physical description area for an incomplete serial (see rule 12.5B1).

Frame 156   Museum should be italicised in the heading in this frame.

Frame 173   Rule 21.35A1 stipulates that a treaty of this type is entered under the heading for the government whose catalogue entry heading is first in English alphabetic order. The second format is therefore the more correct.

Frame 199   Three spaces should have been inserted before 'sound tape reels' in the sample entry for American folklore.

Frame 210   The duration should read (ca. 2 min., 30 sec.) rather than (ca. 2½ min.) - (see rule 6.5B2).

Frame 211   If a note which is not a quotation begins with a numeral then this is spelled out - Appendix C3 - therefore the frequency note should read: Four or 5 issues yearly.

Frame 213   The note of the publisher's number should, more correctly, be preceded by the label name and a colon, i.e. Arcade: ADE C1 (see rule 6.7B19).

    Keen-eyed students may, perhaps, have noticed that the cataloguing of the sound recording is not quite so straightforward as was claimed! A strict interpretation of rule 6.1F1 would require the omission of a person or corporate body from the statement of responsibility area if the participation of the person or body is confined to performance, execution or interpretation. The person or body would then be named in a note (see rule 6.7B6). Such an interpretation might be argued in this instance, giving the entry:

London Symphony Orchestra
    All time classics. - [London] : Arcade, 1973. - 1 sound disc (ca. 60 min.) : 33⅓ rpm, stereo. ; 12 in. - London Symphony Orchestra, Ezra Rachlin, conductor. - Arcade: ADE C1.

Rule 6.1F1 could prove somewhat difficult to apply in practice.

AACR 2

an introduction to the
second edition of
Anglo-American Cataloguing Rules

ERIC J HUNTER MA FLA AMIET
Senior Lecturer
Liverpool Polytechnic

CLIVE BINGLEY
LONDON

LINNET BOOKS
HAMDEN · CONN

FIRST PUBLISHED AS
ANGLO-AMERICAN CATALOGUING RULES 1967:
AN INTRODUCTION
THIS REVISED EDITION PUBLISHED 1979
BY CLIVE BINGLEY LTD
COMMONWEALTH HOUSE, NEW OXFORD STREET, LONDON WC1
SIMULTANEOUSLY PUBLISHED IN THE USA BY LINNET BOOKS
AN IMPRINT OF THE SHOE STRING PRESS INC
995 SHERMAN AVENUE HAMDEN CONNECTICUT 06514
SET IN 10 ON 12 POINT PRESS ROMAN BY ALLSET
PRINTED AND BOUND IN THE UK BY REDWOOD BURN LTD
TROWBRIDGE AND ESHER
COPYRIGHT © ERIC J HUNTER 1979
ALL RIGHTS RESERVED
BINGLEY ISBN: 0-85157-282-0
LINNET ISBN: 0-208-01684-8

Library of Congress Cataloging in Publication Data

Hunter, Eric J
    AACR 2: an introduction to the second edition of
Anglo-American cataloguing rules.

    "First published as Anglo-American cataloguing rules
1967: an introduction"
    Includes index.
    1. Anglo-American cataloguing rules. 2. Descriptive
cataloguing—Programmed instruction. I. Title.
Z694.H85   1979   025.3'2'077   78-23933
ISBN 0-208-01684-8

CONTENTS

ACKNOWLEDGEMENTS

My thanks are due to Ken Bakewell, Joan Bibby and Nicholas Fox, colleagues on the staff of Liverpool Polytechnic, for working through the program in draft form and for their helpful comment and advice.

I am also grateful to the following bodies for permission to reproduce the items noted:

Arcade Records	*All time classics* record label
Longman Group Ltd	Title page of the serial *Teaching geography*
Public Relations Office, Merseyside	Map of *Merseyside after local government reorganisation in 1974*
WORLDS (Western Ohio Regional Library Development System)	Information from WORLDS book-bag

PREFACE

Looking back to the Preface which I wrote for the first edition of this work I was surprised to find that it was not possible to reproduce it verbatim. This is a measure of the developments which have taken place in bibliographical affairs in six short years. Admittedly the first edition took several years to prepare after the publication of AACR 1 in 1967. Even so, however, the slightly longer interval of eleven years between AACR 1 and AACR 2 has seen a vast range of development in descriptive cataloguing.

Whatever might be said in favour of AACR 1, especially when one considers the sixty year gap between it and the 1908 AA rules, it is fair to say that AACR 2 measures an equal step forward. It is important, therefore, that a programmed text of the latest version of the rules be available without delay to place them in perspective for students and others intent on their consideration.

Though those who prepared AACR 2 did not have the benefit of the searching analysis of Seymour Lubetzsky it can be claimed that much of his philosophy still permeates the text. The new rules are a natural extension of AACR 1 and deserve the attention of all concerned to provide improvement in catalogues and information retrieval in the years to come.

It was acknowledged in the Preface to the first edition of Eric Hunter's work that the philosophy of AACR 1 was simple, clear and effective—characteristics which apply even more distinctively to AACR 2. In contrast to its predecessor, it can be claimed for AACR 2, that a single reading will give a clearer picture of the objectives of library catalogues and the means by which they are attained. Nonetheless we must ensure that AACR 2 is applied extensively, despite the inhibiting nature of large data bases, which because of financial strictures may be limited in their contents to the imperfections of past practice.

All that was said of Eric Hunter in the Preface of the previous edition can be repeated here with the addition that he served as a member of the Library Association/British Library Committee for the revision of AACR which met from 1975 -1977. From his experience as a practising cataloguer and as a Senior Lecturer in the Department of Library and Information Studies at Liverpool Polytechnic he has therefore contributed to the new rules. No one could be better qualified to introduce AACR 2 to a larger audience through the medium of a programmed text.

J C DOWNING
Director, Bibliographic Services Division, British Library
Chairman, Cataloguing & Indexing Group, Library Association

INTRODUCTION

The second edition of *Anglo-American cataloguing rules*, hereinafter referred to as AACR 2, continues the precedent set by the first edition in that it is based upon 'conditions' rather than 'cases'. Entries such as 'encyclopedias' will not appear in its index, for the *type* of publication is not considered to be of prime importance. More important are questions such as 'who is primarily responsible for the intellectual or artistic content of an item?' In other words, AACR 2 is not 'enumerative'; it does not attempt to list all the various kinds of publication, but it is based upon a set of principles. An encyclopedia, for example, might be entered under its author, or under its title, etc. Each individual encyclopedia must be treated separately according to the *conditions of authorship or responsibility* appertaining to it. There will, of course, be a few occasions when a particular type of publication represents one—and only one—'condition'. An example is a 'concordance', which is covered by the rule for 'related works', and, in this instance, the type of publication will be found in the index to AACR 2.

AACR 2, however, differs from the first edition (AACR 1) in several very important ways. One major difference is that the first step in the cataloguing of an item is to describe it. With AACR 1, the first step was to choose a heading for the main entry.* Using AACR 2, choice of access points, or headings, *follows* the formulation of a description. One access point is selected as the heading for the main entry.

Having chosen the access points, or the headings for the main entry and for other added (ie secondary) entries, problems regarding the *form* that such headings may take must be resolved and references must be made from forms of headings not used.

* *A main entry is the complete catalogue record of an item, presented in the form by which the entity is to be uniformly identified and cited.*

9

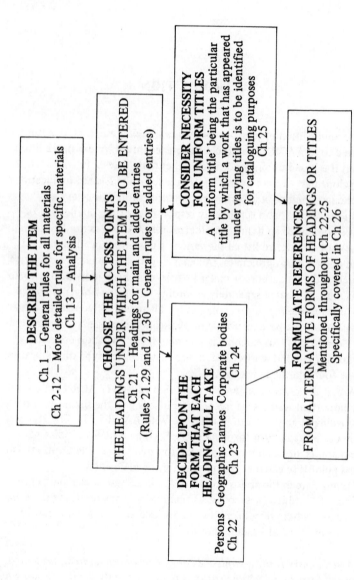

DESCRIBE THE ITEM
Ch 1 – General rules for all materials
Ch 2-12 – More detailed rules for specific materials
Ch 13 – Analysis

CHOOSE THE ACCESS POINTS
THE HEADINGS UNDER WHICH THE ITEM IS TO BE ENTERED
Ch 21 – Headings for main and added entries
(Rules 21.29 and 21.30 – General rules for added entries)

DECIDE UPON THE FORM THAT EACH HEADING WILL TAKE
Persons Geographic names Corporate bodies
Ch 22 Ch 23 Ch 24

CONSIDER NECESSITY FOR UNIFORM TITLES
A 'uniform title' being the particular title by which a work that has appeared under varying titles is to be identified for cataloguing purposes
Ch 25

FORMULATE REFERENCES
FROM ALTERNATIVE FORMS OF HEADINGS OR TITLES
Mentioned throughout Ch 22-25
Specifically covered in Ch 26

Figure 1: Work flowchart for AACR 2

The manner in which AACR 2 tackles these problems may be illustrated in flowchart form, as shown in figure one.

To illustrate more clearly how AACR 2 may be used, let us consider the following item and some of the cataloguing problems that it poses.

THE APPEARANCE OF MAN

by

Pierre Teilhard De Chardin

Translated by J M Cohen

First published under the title

L'Apparition de l'homme

Problems	*Answer provided in* AACR 2 *by*
1 How is the item to be described?	Chapter 1—General rules for description and, if necessary, Chapter 2—Printed monographs, which provides more detailed rules for the particular medium.
2 What access points are to be chosen?	Chapter 21—Choice of access points, specifically rules 21.14—Translations; 21.30K1—Added entries for translators; and 21.30J —Added entries for titles
3 How can the separation, in the catalogue, of the original and the translated titles be overcome?	Chapter 25—Uniform titles. (It should be noted that this is an optional chapter)
4 What is the form of heading to be used for the original author? Is it to be entered under Teilhard de Chardin, De Chardin, or Chardin?	Chapter 22—Headings for persons, specifically rule 22.5C—Compound surnames.
5 What references are to be made from the forms of heading not chosen and from alternative titles?	For compound surnames, indicated in specific rule 22.5C; for uniform titles, indicated in chapter 25. Requirements for references summarised in chapter 26.

It can be seen from the flowchart that AACR 2 attempts to deal *concurrently* with library materials of every kind. This is a further major difference between AACR 1 and AACR 2.

AACR 2 also achieves the distinction of being the first code of rules to be accepted as a uniform standard throughout the English speaking world. There are no variations between the British and North American texts as there were with AACR 1. It is to be officially adopted by the national libraries of Australia, Canada, Great Britain and the United States as from January 1981.

HOW TO USE THIS BOOK

This programmed text is designed to teach the principles underlying AACR 2, rather than a detailed knowledge of the rules themselves. You will need a copy of AACR 2 by you as you work through the program. You should use it as directed and to help solve the set problems.

Lessons and problems are divided into *frames*. These are numbered for easy reference and they must be worked through as instructed.

The course as a whole is divided into a number of separate sections, or *phases*, as indicated on the contents page.

It may be necessary to refer to general reference books from time to time. Every cataloguer must have direct access to sources of information on a variety of topics.

Before turning to phase one and beginning this program, you should read the General Introduction to AACR 2 (sections 0.1 to 0.14).

PHASE ONE

DESCRIPTION

AACR 2 Part I

In this first part of AACR 2, Chapter 1 is a 'General chapter', applicable to all types of materials. This general chapter is followed by a further twelve chapters, all except one of which are concerned with more detailed rules for particular media, ie:

2   Books, pamphlets, etc (printed monographs)
3   Cartographic materials
4   Manuscripts
5   Music
6   Sound recordings
7   Motion pictures and video recordings
8   Graphic materials
9   Machine-readable data files
10 Three-dimensional artefacts and realia
11 Microforms
12 Serials

The exception is the last chapter, chapter 13, which deals with analysis.

Before proceeding to frame 1, read sections 0.21 and 0.22 of the Introduction to Part I of AACR 2. Note that the rules for description in AACR 2 conform to the General International Standard Bibliographic Description—ISBD (G).

FRAME 1

Every item to be catalogued must be described using a standard format. This means that each description must contain the *same basic components*. These must always be cited in the *same order* and be preceded by a *consistent punctuation*. Such standardisation facilitates the local, national and international exchange of materials data and is particularly important in computerised systems. To a machine, *A tale of two cities* and 'Charles Dickens' are simply strings of characters. The computer cannot identify one as the 'title' and the other as the 'author' *unless* it is 'told' which position in a descriptive record each will occupy and how each will be introduced.

 Proceed to next frame

FRAME 2

To achieve the standardisation referred to in the previous frame, the description is divided into the following areas (see rule 1.0B) always cited in the order shown:

Title and statement of responsibility	1
Edition	2
Material (or type of publication) specific details	3
Publication, distribution, etc	4
Physical description	5
Series	6
Note(s)	7
Standard number and terms of availability	8

 It is not necessary for *all* of these areas to be present in every case. An item may not, for instance, be included in a series or have a standard number. Similarly, a note may not always be required. One area, the 'material (or type of publication) specific details' area, is, in fact, only used for two types of material—maps and serials.

 The number given on the right is the relevant rule number for that particular area. These numbers are used mnemonically so that rule 1.1 will deal with the recording of the title in general terms, rule 2.1 will deal more specifically with the recording of the title of a printed monograph, rule 6.1 with the recording of the title or a sound recording and so on.

 Proceed to next frame

FRAME 3

The first frame referred to three major conditions which must be satisfied in order to achieve standardisation of cataloguing descriptions. Can you remember what these conditions are?

Turn to frame 31 for the answer.

FRAME 4

Each description must contain the same basic components and these must be cited in a consistent order. The basic descriptive areas were listed in frame 2. Each of these areas may be further divided into constituent elements, for example the 'publication, distribution, etc' area could contain elements such as the place of publication, publisher and date of publication (see rule 1.4).

Attempt to identify the major elements which together make up the 'physical description' area by referring to Chapter 1 of AACR 2 and by using frame 2 to find the relevant rule number within this chapter.

Turn to frame 29 for the answer.

FRAME 5

With regard to the third condition for standardisation, which is a designated punctuation, each area other than the first is preceded by a full stop, space, dash, space (. —). Alternatively, an area can begin a new paragraph.

Elements within areas must also be divided by consistent punctuation. For example, a statement of responsibility is always preceded by a diagonal slash, eg:

A tale of two cities / Charles Dickens (see rule 1.1A1).

What punctuation separates place of publication, publisher and date within the 'publication, etc' area?

Turn to frame 40 for the answer

FRAME 6

Information to be included in the description is extracted from 'prescribed' sources. (Information taken from outside the prescribed sources must always be enclosed in square brackets). Such sources are noted in a section of the first rule of every chapter (usually numbered .0B, ie: 2.0B, 3.0B, 4.0B, etc). By referring to the relevant rules, find the chief sources of information for:

a)   a printed monograph
b)   a sound disc
c)   a serial

   If you are not sure how a monograph and/or a serial may be defined, refer first to the glossary (Appendix D of AACR 2) before turning to frame 30 for the answer.

FRAME 7

One or more sources of information are also prescribed for each area within the descriptive rules specifically related to a particular medium. What sources of information, therefore, may be used for obtaining physical details relating to a printed monograph?

   Turn to frame 26 for the answer.

FRAME 8

As indicated in previous frames, the basic descriptive areas, with the required preceding punctuation, are:

   Title and statement of responsibility. — Edition. — Material (or type of publication) specific details. — Publication, distribution, etc. — Physical description. — (Series). — Note(s). — Standard number.

Inserting the relevant, basic constituent elements for a printed monograph into these areas, together with the required punctuation, would amend this layout to:

Title / Statement of responsibility. — Edition. — Place of publication : Publisher, Date. — Pagination : Illustration ;   Size (i.e. height in cm). — (Series). — Note(s). — Standard number.

(continued)

Substituting details relating to an actual item would give:

Modern mathematics at Ordinary Level / by L. Harwood Clarke. – 2nd ed. – London : Heinemann Educational, 1970. – ix, 212p. : ill. ; 23 cm. – (Heinemann's modern mathematics series). – With answers. – ISBN 0-435-50253-0.

This is the basic descriptive layout for a printed monograph. Note that paragraphing could replace the 'full stop, space, dash, space' punctuation. Paragraphing is often utilised for the physical description area, the notes area and for the standard number, eg:

Modern mathematics at Ordinary Level / by L. Harwood Clarke. – 2nd ed. – London : Heinemann Educational, 1970.
ix, 212 p. : ill. ; 23 cm. – (Heinemann's modern mathematics series).
With answers.
ISBN 0-435-50253-0.

Whether paragraphing is adopted or not, and to what degree it is adopted, will depend upon the 'in-house' style of the particular cataloguing agency. As it is a variable option, paragraphing will not be used throughout the remainder of this text; layout will conform to the first of the examples given above. Using this sample, basic layout, and without referring to AACR 2, produce a description for the following item:

Small garden series

IMPROVING YOUR GARDEN
by
Oliver Dawson

London   Pan

Revised edition
1972

ISBN 0 330 02896 0

The previous edition was published in 1967 by Collingridge of Feltham as *Making the most of your garden*. The book has 10 pages numbered in Roman followed by 165 numbered in Arabic. It is illustrated and is 18 cm high.
When you have completed this description, turn to frame 41

FRAME 9

Basic layouts for other media, conforming, as they must, to the rules in the general chapter, are very similar to that for printed monographs but obviously there will be differences in detail, especially where physical description is concerned.

Here are one or two examples:

> Rates and services : how you pay and what you get / prepared by Pictorial Charts Educational Trust. — Rev. ed. — London : P.C.E.T., [196–?]. — 1 wallchart : col. ; 76 x 101 cm. folded to 19 x 26 cm.

Compare this description with that of the printed monograph given in frame 8. Note that only the following areas are present in this instance:

> Title and statement of responsibility. — Edition. — Publication, distribution, etc. — Physical description.

Series, notes and standard number areas were not required but of course they may well be required in descriptions relating to other wallcharts.

The following description of a serial contains a title area, publication area, physical description area and a note, ie the frequency. Again certain areas, for example a series, and certain elements within areas, for example a statement of responsibility, are not needed in the particular instance although they may well be needed for other serials. Note particularly that, for a serial, use is made of the 'material (or type of publication) specific details' area (see frame 2). In the case of a serial, this area consists of a numerical and chronological designation (see rule 12.3), eg Vol. 1, no. 1 (Jan 1970) — (the numeric designation could, of course, be 'alphabetic' in certain instances).

> Home beer and winemaking. — Vol. 1, no. 1 (Jan. 1970)-   . — Wirral : Foremost Press, 1970-   . — v. : ill. ; 28 cm. — Monthly. — ISSN 0041-090X.

Lastly, here is a description of a game (for which the relevant specific chapter is Chapter 10 'Three dimensional artefacts and realia'). List the areas present in this description and those which are not. Turn to frame 24 for the correct answer.

> Kan-u-go : the crossword card game. — Leeds : Jarvis, Porter, 1934. — 1 game (58 lettered cards and 2 Kan-u-go cards) ; in box, 8 x 12 x 2 cm. — For two to seven players and also Kan-u-go alone patience. — Instruction booklet (28p.) in lid.

FRAME 10

The sample descriptions for various media considered in the previous frames have been included to provide some indication of the overall objectives of Part 1 of AACR 2. Although such basic layouts are useful from this point of view, it must be appreciated that these were simple, illustrative examples. In practice, the cataloguer will encounter many hundreds of different, and sometimes very difficult, problems. For the solutions to such problems, the appropriate rules in the general chapter and in the chapter relating to the particular medium should be referred to.

Here is an example of a common cataloguing problem. A publisher may well operate from more than one place and these places will be shown in a published item, eg:

HAMLYN

London New York Sydney Toronto

1974

Which of these places is to be included in the publication area? Guidance will be found in rule 1.4B8. Refer to this rule and, assuming that the item is a printed monograph, also examine rule 2.4B and decide what would be included in the publication area for this item by a cataloguing agency in Canada.

Turn to frame 32 for the answer.

FRAME 11

Problems related to publication are not confined to printed monographs. Refer to Chapter 6 and attempt to discover what should be included in the publication area for a sound recording which bears on its label both the name of the publishing company (CBS Records of London) and also a brand name (Epic).

Turn to frame 35 for the answer.

FRAME 12

Having considered, in general terms, the contents of a description, the individual constituent areas will now be examined in more detail. This will provide an indication of the way in which AACR 2 approaches some of the every day problems that may arise.

The first area is the 'title and statement of responsibility' area (see rule 1.1). A title is transcribed from an item exactly as to wording, order and spelling but not necessarily as to capitalisation (see Appendix A of AACR 2), punctuation (see rule 1.1A1) and, quite obviously, typeface.
For example:

AN ECONOMIC AND SOCIAL HISTORY

OF BRITAIN SINCE 1700

would become:

An economic and social history of Britain since 1700

The general capitalisation rule for titles in the English language is that the first letters of all proper names are capitalised, otherwise lower case letters are used except for the first letter of a title. Hence only the first letter 'A' and the 'B' of Britain are capitalised in the above example.

Any additional unit of title information, for example a subtitle, is preceded by a colon, eg:

The two Elizabeths : a jubilee concert

A parallel title is preceded by an equals sign, eg:

Thumbelina = Tommelise

Long titles may be abridged but only if this can be done without loss of essential information. The first five words must never be omitted. Any omissions are indicated by the mark of omission, ie, three dots (. . .) (see rule 1.0C).

If an item lacks the prescribed sources of information from which a title may be extracted, a title must be supplied from, in order of preference, the rest of the item, or a reference source, or elsewhere. Such a supplied title must be enclosed in square brackets, eg:

[Wooden chair]

Now attempt to transcribe the following title:

OUT OF THE DINOSAURS
THE EVOLUTION OF THE NATIONAL LENDING
LIBRARY FOR SCIENCE AND TECHNOLOGY

Turn to frame 38 for the answer.

FRAME 13

Imagine that you are cataloguing a banana! What would the title statement be?

Turn to frame 36 for the answer.

FRAME 14

An optional inclusion, following the title proper, is a 'general material designation'. This consists of a term chosen from a supplied list enclosed within square brackets (see rule 1.1C), for example:

Hamlet [text]

Hamlet [motion picture]

Hamlet [sound recording]

Sir Winston Churchill [sound recording] : selected speeches

As this is an *optional* rule, it will not be used in the remainder of the examples in this text but remember that the rule does exist if such material designations are required.

Proceed to the next frame

FRAME 15

Statements of responsibility, which are preceded by a diagonal slash, are recorded in the form that they appear in or on the item (see rule 1.1F), eg:

Best of ol' blue eyes / Frank Sinatra

An economic and social history of Britain since 1700 / by Michael W. Flinn

Suspended structures / British Constructional Steelwork Association

Roman Britain / research and text by Colin Barham

The Oxford book of English verse / chosen and edited by Sir Arthur Quiller-Couch

Data interchange on industry-compatible tapes / M. Visvalingam, M.J. Norman, R. Sheehan

An explanatory word or short phrase may be added, if desired, when the relationship to the title is other than that of simple 'authorship', eg:

Baijun ballads / [collected by] Chet Williams

When there is more than one statement of responsibility, statements subsequent to the first are introduced by a semi-colon, eg:

24

Flowering house plants month by month / by Jack Kramer ;
drawings by Andrew R. Addkison

La vie parisienne : operetta in three acts / Jacques Offenbach ;
music adapted and arranged by Ronald Hanmer ; new book and
lyrics by Phil Park

Usually, academic degrees and titles of honour or address (except for
titles of nobility and British titles of honour) are omitted but there are
exceptions to this principle and rule 1.1F7 should be carefully studied.

When a statement of responsibility relates to more than three persons
or bodies, all but the first of these are omitted (see rule 1.1F5). The
omission must be indicated (by . . .) and 'et al' must be added in square
brackets, eg:

America's radical right / Raymond Wolfinger . . . [et al]

If no formal statement of responsibility appears in an item then
AACR 2 instructs (rule 1.1F2) that one is not to be constructed nor
extracted from the text of the item.

Study rule 1.1 of AACR 2 and then transcribe the titles and statements of responsibility for the following items:

a)   THE HOME MEDICAL ENCYCLOPEDIA

by

David Forsyth, M.R.C.P.

b)   FLIGHT OF FANCY
A History of Aviation

by

J.W. Small   P. Winter   S. Goody
T. Wilson

Turn to frame 34 for the answers

FRAME 16

The edition statement is transcribed as found in the item but standard abbreviations (see Appendix B of AACR 2) and numerals (see Appendix C of AACR 2) are used instead of words, eg:

    2nd ed.

    [Rev. ed.]

    3e ed.

When a statement of responsibility relates only to particular editions and not to *all* editions of an item, then it must be included in this area, eg:

    Explaining the atom / by Selig Hecht. — Rev. and with additional chapters / by Eugene Rabinowitch

An issue statement may be given in addition to an edition statement if the reissue contains changes (see rule 1.2D), eg:

    5th ed. Repr. with additions and amendments

Which rule should be consulted if a problem arises regarding the edition statement relating to an art reproduction?

Turn to frame 27 for the answer

FRAME 17

The 'material (or type of publication) specific details' area is only used for serials and maps. Its use for serials has already been explained (frame 9). For maps, it is used to present mathematical data, particularly the scale. This is given as a representative fraction expressed as a ratio and preceded by the word 'scale', eg:

    Scale 1 : 63,360

Examine rules 1.3, 3.3 and 12.3. Then give the numerical and chronological designations that would appear in this area for a serial which began publication with volume one in 1949 and ceased publication with volume fourteen in 1962.

Turn to frame 25 for the answer.

FRAME 18

The 'publication, distribution, etc' area has already been partially explained in previous frames. The basic elements consist of the place of publication, publisher and date, eg:

    New York : Harper, 1956

Generally, only the first named place of publication and first named publisher are included but other, subsequent places or publishers may be cited if given prominence by the layout of the source of information or if located in the home country of the cataloguing agency.

For example.

New York : McGraw Hill

in a United States library catalogue could well appear as:

New York ; London : McGraw Hill

in the UK.

The publisher is given in the briefest form in which it can be understood and identified internationally, eg:

Norman Price (Publishers) Ltd

would be given as:

N. Price

If a publisher is named in the title and statement of responsibility area, it is given in the publication area in an abbreviated form. The wallchart example in frame 9 illustrates this rule.

The date to be given is the date of the edition, thus an attempt is made to convey to the catalogue user the currency of the information in an item. The date of a re-issue of an edition is only to be given if the re-issue is specified in the edition area (see frame 16). For example, if the fifth edition of an item is issued in 1967 and is then reprinted with additions and amendments and re-issued in 1972, then the edition area is recorded as:

5th ed. Repr. with additions and amendments

and the date is given as:

1972

A copyright date or a date of manufacture may be given if the publication, distribution, etc date is unknown.

No matter how approximate, a date must *always* be given. Even [19——?], which means 'probably twentieth century', is better than no date at all.

In some cases, the name of the publisher may be unknown, or even irrelevant. If this is so, the place and name of the manufacturer can be given if found in or on the item. These details must be enclosed in parentheses, eg:

[Wooden chair] . — 1881 (Chiswick : Morris & Co.)

Examine rule 1.4. An item was first published in 1950. A second edition was published in 1958 and a third edition in 1964. The latter was reprinted in 1966. What date would appear in the publication area of the catalogue description for this reprint?

Turn to frame 37 for the answer.

FRAME 19

The four major elements of the physical description area, as indicated in frame 25, are:

Extent of item (including specific material designation)
Other physical details
Dimensions
Accompanying material

The first three elements are obviously the most important. With regard to punctuation, 'Other physical details' are preceded by a colon and 'dimensions' by a semi-colon. Here are a few examples of physical descriptions of various media:

Extent	:	Other physical details	;	Dimensions
531 p.	:	ill. (some col.)	;	25 cm.
xi, 101 p.	:	ill. (woodcuts)	;	33 cm. (fol.)
1 map	:	col., plastic	;	26 x 52 cm.
[1] leaf	:	parchment	;	35 x 45 cm.
1 vocal score (55p.)	:	ill.	;	24 cm.
1 sound disc (45 min.)	:	33 1/3 rpm, stereo	;	12 in.
1 film reel (30 min.)	:	sd., col.	;	16 mm.
1 art original	:	oil on canvas	;	45 x 60 cm.
1 data file (30000 logical records)				
1 vase	:	porcelain, white	;	30cm. high
v.	:	ill.	;	25 cm.
1 microfiche	:	ill.	;	10 x 15 cm.

Note that a specific material designation is not necessary in every case, eg in the first example, which relates to a printed monograph. The specific material designation for a printed serial is 'v'.

Note also that these examples are merely illustrative of the many possible variations and rule .5 in the general chapter and in the appropriate chapter for each medium must be consulted for a full range of examples.

Accompanying material may be recorded in the physical description area and, if so, it is preceded by a plus sign, eg:

+ 12 slides
+ 1 sound disc

Optionally, a fuller description may be provided in accordance with the general rules for the particular medium, eg:

+ 12 slides : col.

+ 1 sound disc (30 min. : 33 1/3 rpm, mono. ; 12 in.)

Formulate a physical description for a sound recording made on a cassette tape. The cassette dimensions are 3 7/8 x 2½ inches. The tape width is 1/8 inch. The playing speed is 1 7/8 inches per second and the playing time is 60 minutes. The recording is in stereo.

Turn to frame 28 for the answer

FRAME 20

The series area, like other areas, is preceded by a full stop, space, dash, space but, unlike other areas, the series statement is enclosed in parentheses, eg:

(Marketing management series)

Statements of responsibility appearing in the chief source of information are given if they are considered to be necessary for the identification of the series, eg:

(Technical memorandum / Beach Erosion Board)

The number of an item within a series is recorded in the terms given in the item, eg:

(The library series ; 1)

(Cahiers d'histoire ; no.20)

If the ISSN of the series is given in the item, then this also is recorded, eg:

(An economic study, ISSN 0307-4919 ; no.36)

Read through rule 1.6. What information would be included in the series area for an item which is stated to be both No.434 of the World Health Organisation's Technical report series and No.81 of the Food and Agricultural Organisation's Agricultural studies?

Turn to frame 33 for the answer.

FRAME 21

Notes are intended to amplify or clarify the more formal elements of the description. They may take many forms. Examples of notes are:

Bibliography : p.203-215

Previous ed. : Harmondsworth : Penguin, 1950

Contents: Rusty bugles / Sumner Locke Elliott — We find the bunyip / Ray Mathew — The well / Jack McKinney

Also available in 16 mm. format

For children aged 9-12

Based on the life of Florence Nightingale

Summary: Pictures the highlights of the play 'Julius Caesar' using photographs of an actual production

Other examples of a wide variety of notes will be found in rule .7 of each chapter of Part 1 of AACR 2.

In general, notes should be as brief as possible (see rule 1.7A3) and should not repeat information already given in an entry.

Notes are particularly important where media which cannot be 'browsed', eg films, is concerned and they should be freely used. A summary of the content and subject of an item is often essential.

Notes are presented in an order as laid down in rule 1.7B. This is basically the order of the areas of the description, ie notes on the title, notes on the statement of responsibility, notes on the edition, etc, but preceded by general notes on the nature, scope, form and language of an item.

You are cataloguing a reproduction of a painting, the original of which is known to be in London's National Portrait Gallery. Is it necessary to include this information in the description and, if so, which form of note from those listed below would you choose?

This is a reproduction of the original which is located in the National Portrait Gallery.

Original National Portrait Gallery, London.

Turn to frame 39 for the answer

FRAME 22

In the standard number area, the ISBN (International Standard Book Number), ISSN (International Standard Serial Number), or any other internationally agreed number of an item is to be given, eg:

ISBN 0-552-67587-3

ISSN 0002-9769

CBS 86010

In the case of a serial, the 'key title' (see definition in Glossary—Appendix D of AACR 2) is given following the ISSN if it is readily available.

Optionally, the terms of availability, including the price, of an item may also be given, eg:

: £6.75

: For hire

: Free to members

Proceed to next frame

FRAME 23

Except for 'Analysis' (see Phase 7), this completes our brief study of Part One of AACR 2, although one further point needs to be made. This is that AACR 2 prescribes three levels of detail in the description, according to the requirements of individual libraries and cataloguing agencies. In general, the rules themselves constitute a maximum set of information, that is a *third* level of description. For those agencies not requiring this amount of detail, rule 1.0D outlines, in addition, first and second levels. The first level, for example, includes:

Title proper / first statement of responsibility, if different from the main entry heading in form or number or if there is no main entry heading. – Edition statement. – Material (or type of publication) specific detail. – First publisher, etc., date of publication, etc. – Extent of item. Note(s). – Standard number.

In effect this constitutes a minimum level and the second level, which adds further elements, constitutes an intermediate level.
Rule 1.0D should be examined.

At this point, it might be helpful, before proceeding to phase two, to read through the remainder of the Introduction to Part I of AACR 2 (sections 0.23 to 0.29). This will not only act as a revision exercise but will provide a further, general review of this first part of the rules.
Phase two follows frame 41.

FRAME 24

The areas present in the description of the game are:
Title area. – Publication area. – Physical description. – Notes
There are no edition, series, and standard number areas in this instance.
Proceed to frame 10

FRAME 25

The answer is (see rule 12.3F):
Vol.1 (1949)-v.14 (1962)
Proceed to frame 18

FRAME 26

Rule 2.0B2 instructs that the whole publication may be used as a source of information for physical details relating to a printed monograph.

Proceed to frame 8

FRAME 27

The relevant rule relating to the edition statement for an art reproduction is 8.2, where 8 is the relevant chapter for graphic materials and 2 is the number of the rule within this chapter for the edition area. It should be remembered, however, that rule 2 of the general chapter (ie rule 1.2) is also applicable.

Proceed to frame 17

FRAME 28

The physical description should be:

    1 sound cassette (60 min.) : 1 7/8 ips, stereo.

The relevant chapter is Chapter 6, 'Sound recordings', and the relevant rule 6.5. If you were incorrect re-examine these rules. Note that the word 'sound' could be dropped if it has already appeared in a general material designation (see frame 14). Note also that the cassette dimensions and the tape width are omitted because they are standard (see rule 6.5D5).

Where 'physical description' is concerned, mention must be made of 'multi-media' items, ie those that are made up of two or more components of differing material types. If such an item has one predominant component it is described in terms of that component; the subsidiary components are treated as accompanying materials and recorded in the physical description area, as indicated in frame 19, or given in a note (see the description of the game in frame 9).*

However, it may well be that a 'multi-media' item has no predominant component. In this case, the extent of each part, or group of parts, in each class of material must be recorded, followed, if necessary, by a

---

* *Accompanying material may also be recorded in a separate entry or in a multi-level description (see rules 1.5E1 and 1.10D). Multi-level description will be dealt with at a later stage of this program.*

separate physical description for each part or group of parts, eg for a tape-slide presentation:

     25 slides : col.

     1 sound cassette (15 min.) : 3¾ ips., mono.

If an item consists of a large number of heterogeneous materials, a general description of the extent such as:

     33 various pieces

may be given.

    Items made up of several types of material are dealt with in rule 1.10. Examine this rule and then proceed to frame 20.

FRAME 29

Rule 1.5 indicates that the major elements of the physical description area are:

Extent of item (including specific material designation), eg: 24 photographs

Other physical details, eg: col.

Dimensions, eg: 13 x 8 cm.

Accompanying material, eg: + booklet

    Proceed to frame 5

FRAME 30

The chief sources of information are:

a)   For a printed monograph—the title page (see rule 2.OB1)

b)   For a sound disc—the label (see rule 6.OB1)

c)   For a serial—the title page of the first volume or issue or, failing this, the title page of the first volume or issue which is available (see rule 12.OB1)

    Proceed to frame 7

FRAME 31

To achieve standardisation, each description must consist of the *same basic components*. These components must be cited in the *same order* and be preceded by a *consistent punctuation*.

    Proceed to frame 4

FRAME 32

The answer that you should have is:

London ; Toronto : Hamlyn, 1974

If you are incorrect, return to rule 1.4B8 and re-examine it, particularly noting the first example.

Then proceed to frame 11

FRAME 33

Rule 1.6J1 is the relevant rule and proceeding as instructed therein would give the following separate series statements:

(Technical report series / World Health Organisation ; no. 434)
(Agricultural studies / Food and Agricultural Organisation ; no. 81)

Proceed to frame 21

FRAME 34

The title and statements of responsibility should be:
a)   The home medical encyclopedia / by David Forsyth
b)   Flight of fancy : a history of aviation / by J.W. Small . . . [et al.]

Note that the titles are transcribed exactly as to wording, order and spelling but not as to capitalisation. Note that the statements of responsibility are recorded as given in the item but that the author's qualifications, etc are omitted and that when there are more than three persons in a statement of responsibility all but the first of these is omitted. The latter omission is indicated by three dots and 'et al' is added in square brackets.

Proceed to frame 16

FRAME 35

The answer, provided by rule 6.4D2, is:

London : Epic

Proceed to frame 12

FRAME 36
The title statement would be:

[Banana]

Note that the title is enclosed in square brackets, denoting that it has been supplied from outside the prescribed sources of information.

Proceed to frame 14

FRAME 37
The answer is 1964. If you were incorrect, look again at rules 1.4F1 and 1.4F3. The date must be the date of the edition named in the edition area. This would be the 3rd ed. There would be no need to specify the reprint in this area and the date of the reprint need not, therefore, be included in the publication area.

Proceed to frame 19

FRAME 38
The title transcription should be:

Out of the dinosaurs : the evolution of the National Lending
Library for Science and Technology

If you were wrong, read through frame 12 and rule 1.1 again before proceeding to frame 13

FRAME 39
This is information of importance to many catalogue users and it should be included. The first note, however, is far too lengthy, repeats information probably already given in the earlier parts of the description (ie reproduction) and yet fails to say in which National Portrait Gallery the painting is located. The brief, but informative note which should have been selected (see rule 8.7B8) is:

Original National Portrait Gallery, London.

Proceed to frame 22

FRAME 40

The basic punctuation in the publication area (see rule 1.4A1) is:

    place : publisher, date

eg: London : Collins, 1964

Note that each mark of prescribed punctuation is preceded by a space and followed by a space, except for a comma, full stop and opening and closing parentheses or square brackets.

Proceed to frame 6

FRAME 41

Check your answer against the following correct version:

> Improving your garden / by Oliver Dawson. — Rev. ed. — London : Pan, 1972. — x, 165 p. : ill. ; 18 cm. — (Small garden series). — Previous ed. published as: Making the most of your garden. Feltham : Collingridge, 1967. — ISBN 0-330-02896-0.

It is likely that most, if not all, of your entry is correct, except perhaps that your note may be differently worded but this is a relatively minor point at this stage.

Certain abbreviations (ed. for edition, rev. for revised and ill. for illustrated) have been used. A full list of permitted abbreviations, together with an indication of the parts of the entry in which they may be used will be found in Appendix B of AACR 2.

A series statement, as indicated, is enclosed in parentheses; series statements will be dealt with further in a later frame.

Proceed to frame 9

PHASE TWO

CHOICE OF ACCESS POINTS

AACR 2 Chapter 21

This is the first chapter of Part II of AACR. In each of the chapters in this part, general rules precede special rules. Where no specific rule exists for a special problem, the more general rules are to be applied. A further point to be stressed is that the rules in Part II apply to *all* library materials.

The introduction to Part II (20.1 to 20.4) should be read before proceeding with this phase

FRAME 42

Having described an item, *headings* are normally added in order to create catalogue entries. *Headings* provide *access points* in the catalogue. A heading may be a word, name or phrase; it appears at the beginning of the entry and fixes the place of the entry in the catalogue as well as grouping related entries together.

One possible access point is, of course, the title proper of an item and, in this instance, it becomes unnecessary to add a heading, entry being made under the first words of the description.

There is one other addition which may be made to a description—a *uniform title*. Uniform titles will be defined, and their use described, in a later phase.

The following description was used as an example in frame 8:

> Modern mathematics at Ordinary Level / by L. Harwood Clarke. — 2nd ed. — London : Heinemann Educational, 1970. — ix, 212 p. : ill.; 23 cm. — (Heinemann's modern mathematics series). — With answers. — ISBN 0-435-50253-0.

Possible headings which could be added to this description to provide access points are:

The person responsible for the work: The heading for L. Harwood Clarke
The series: Heinemann's modern mathematics series

A further possible access point would be:

The title: Modern mathematics at Ordinary Level

What then, might be selected as the headings or access points for the following item?

> The free library : its history and present condition / John J. Ogle. — London : Allen, 1897. — xix, 344 p. ; 20 cm. — (The library series).

Turn to frame 72 for the answer

FRAME 43

The rules for determining the choice of access points in Chapter 21 also give instructions for the choice of one of these access points as the *main entry* heading. A main entry is that entry where the fullest information is found, presented in a form by which an item can be identified and cited. Other entries then become *added* entries and the headings related to those entries are referred to as added entry headings.

Proceed to next frame.

The main entry heading consists of the name of a *person*, the name of a *corporate body*, or a *title*. The basic rule for determining which of these is to be selected is 21.1.

In the case of the names of *persons*, AACR 2 is primarily concerned with the responsibility for the intellectual or artistic content of an item (rule 21.1A). Is there only one person responsible? or is responsibility shared? in which case is there one person principally responsible? etc. Like AACR 1, AACR 2 is, therefore, concerned with *conditions* of responsibility or authorship.

AACR 2 defines a *corporate body* as an organisation or a group of persons that is identified by a particular name and that acts, or may act, as an entity (rule 21.1B). Entry under such bodies is restricted to works which fall into one of the following categories:

a) those of an administrative nature dealing with the corporate body itself

b) legal and governmental works of certain types

c) works which record the collective thought of a body (eg reports of commissions or committees and official statements of position on external policy)

d) those works which report the collective activity of a conference, expedition, or event which falls within the definition of a corporate body and is openly named in the item being catalogued

e) sound recordings, films and videorecordings resulting from the collective activity of a performing group as a whole where the responsibility of the group goes beyond that of mere performance.

A work is entered under its *title* (rule 21.1C) when:

1) the personal authorship is unknown, diffuse, or indeterminable

2) it is a collection or a work produced under editorial direction

3) it emanates from a corporate body but does not fall into one or more of the categories a) to e) above and is not of personal authorship

4) it is accepted as a sacred scripture by a religious group.

Examine this basic rule and decide what the main entry heading for each of the following items would be:

a)   POPULAR PET KEEPING

by

P.M. Soderberg

b)   **BRITISH MUSEUM**

CATALOGUE OF PERSIAN MANUSCRIPTS

c)   **STREET MAP OF FORMBY**

Designed by

Forward Publicity Ltd.

d)   **LIBRARY ASSISTANT**

The Journal of the
Library Assistants' Association

Turn to frame 81 for the answers

FRAME 45
Rule 21.2 gives instructions for dealing with changes of title. A definition
of what can be regarded as a change of title is provided and, basically,
monographs and serials which may be considered to have changed their
titles, in accordance with this definition, have separate main entries
made for each change.

Examine this rule. Do you consider that the example included in
frame 8, *Improving your garden*, which was previously published as
Making the most of your garden, constitutes a *change of title proper*
according to the definition included therein?

Turn to frame 69 for the answer

FRAME 46
Rule 21.3 is concerned with changes of persons or bodies responsible
for a work.

For monographs which have been modified by a person or corporate
body other than the person or body under which the original edition
was entered, reference is made to later rules (21.9-21.23) which are
specifically related to this problem, eg 21.10 Adaptations, 21.12 Revisions, etc. These rules will be dealt with later in this program (frame
60 onwards).

Where there is a change of responsibility between parts of a multipart
monograph, the item is entered under the heading appropriate to the

first part unless a person or body responsible for later parts predominates (rule 21.3A2).

Where serials are concerned, rule 21.3B lays down two conditions of change of responsibility which necessitate a new entry for the serial, even if the title proper remains the same. The conditions are:

1) If the name of a person or corporate body under which a serial is entered changes.
2) If the main entry for a serial is under a personal or corporate heading and the person or corporate body responsible for the serial changes.

The *Library assistant* began publication in 1898, the responsible body being the Library Assistants' Association. This body changed its name to the Association of Assistant Librarians in 1922. Would a new entry be required for the serial according to the provisions of rule 21.3?

In 1953, the *Library assistant* changed its title to *Assistant librarian.* Would a new main entry be needed for this change, in accordance with the provisions of rule 21.2?

Turn to frame 85 for the answers

FRAME 47

As was noted in frame 44, AACR 2 is concerned with *conditions* of responsibility or authorship. The relevant rules for dealing with particular conditions can be ascertained by an examination of the 'Table of contents' on page 279 of the code. An examination of this table will reveal, for instance, that rule 21.4 deals with works for which a single person or corporate body is responsible; rule 21.5 deals with works of unknown or uncertain authorship; rule 21.6 deals with works of shared responsibility; and so on. For more detailed guidance, the index to AACR 2 should be consulted. To use this index, you must not look under, for example, literary forms but under kinds of responsibility, eg single personal authorship.

With this in mind, what would you look up in the index to AACR to find the appropriate rules for determining authorship responsibility for the following items?

a)   ENCYCLOPAEDIA OF WORLD COOKERY

Elizabeth Campbell

b) FERODO LIMITED

Friction materials for engineers

Turn to frame 74 for the answers

FRAME 48

Works for which a single person or corporate body is responsible are dealt with in rule 21.4. A work, collection of works or selections from a work or works by one personal author is to be entered under the heading for that person whether named in the work or not. A work, collection of works, or selections from a work or works emanating from one corporate body is to be entered under the heading for the body *if* the work or collection falls into one or more of the categories given in rule 21.1B2 (see frame 44).

Study the examples *Encyclopaedia of world cookery* and *Friction materials for engineers* included in the previous frame. According to rule 21.4 would main entry be made under the person and corporate body responsible respectively for each item?

Turn to frame 76 for the answer

FRAME 49

Rule 21.4 also includes instructions for dealing with works wrongly or fictiously attributed to a person or corporate body; entry is made under the actual person or body responsible if known, otherwise entry is under title (rule 21.4C). In the case of entry under a corporate body, the relevant work must, of course, fall into the categories given in rule 21.1B2 as noted in the previous frame and in frame 44.

Works by heads of state, high government officials, popes, and other high ecclesiastical officials are dealt with in rule 21.4D. *Official* communications of such people are entered under the corporate heading for the official and not under the personal heading (rule 21.4D1). All other works (21.4D2) and *collections* of official communications by *one* person (rule 21.4D3) are entered under the personal heading.

Study rules 21.4C and 21.4D. Take particular note of the examples contained therein. Note also that, having chosen the corporate heading for an official or a personal heading as the heading for a main entry, added entries or references are made for the heading not chosen.

43

What would the main entry heading be for the following item?

THE OFFICIAL PAPERS OF WILLIAM V. S. TUBMAN
PRESIDENT OF THE REPUBLIC OF LIBERIA

Would any added entries be necessary?
Turn to frame 73 for the answer

FRAME 50
In solving the problem in the frames above, it will have been noted that rule 21.4 also gives instructions for making added entries. Remember that this chapter of AACR 2 is concerned with choice of access points. It follows, therefore, that specific rules will include directions for making added as well as main entry headings. However, the prime concern is with choice of main entry headings and the remainder of this phase will confine itself to this consideration. We will return, in the next phase, to a study of added entries.

Proceed to next frame.

If directed to read this frame again, proceed to phase three, following frame 86.

FRAME 51
There are bound to be occasions when the person or body responsible for a work remains unknown or uncertain. Rule 21.5 covers this eventuality.

Examine this rule, noting that it includes works by groups which lack a name, eg unnamed conferences. Note also that if reference sources indicate that a person is the probable author of a work, entry is under the heading for that person, and if a work falling into one or more of the categories given in 21.1B2 probably emanates from a particular corporate body, entry is under the heading for that body.

Choose main entry headings for the following items:

a)   An anonymous work entitled:

THE CHRISTMAS ANTHOLOGY

b)   Papers presented to a conference of historians of science entitled:

JOHN DALTON AND THE PROGRESS OF SCIENCE

Turn to frame 71 for the answers

FRAME 52

There may well be more than one person or body responsible for a work. They could have a similar relationship to the item, for example they could have written or created it together. This is *shared* authorship or responsibility. When a different relationship exists, for example the work of one person revised by another person, then this is responsibility of *mixed* character, ie an original author and a reviser.

What condition of responsibility is represented by the following item?

THREE PROBLEMS IN FACTORY PLANNING

by

R.F. Baldwin and G.W. Everett

Turn to frame 83 for the answer

FRAME 53

Shared responsibility is dealt with in rule 21.6 of AACR 2. Basically, if a *principal* responsibility is indicated, either by wording or layout, then entry is made under the heading for this *principal* person or body. Otherwise, if there are two or three responsible persons or bodies, main entry is made under the one named first and if there are more than three persons or bodies responsible, main entry is under title.

It may well be that *principal* responsibility is attributed to two or three persons or bodies. In this case entry is made under the heading for the first named of these.

Examine rule 21.6. Under what heading would the main entry for the example cited in the previous frame, *Three problems in factory planning*, appear?

Turn to frame 67 for the answer

FRAME 54

Again referring to rule 21.6, choose a main entry heading for the following work:

THE STORY OF THE WORLD'S WORSHIP

by

FRANK S. DOBBINS

assisted by
S. Wells Williams and Isaac Hall

Turn to frame 80 for the answer

FRAME 55

On the basis of what you have learned so far, choose a main entry heading for the following book:

THE MAKING OF THE WEST INDIES

by

F.R. Augier   S.C. Gordon
D.G. Hall   M. Reckord

Turn to frame 77 for the answer

FRAME 56

Many works of multiple authorship are produced under the direction of an editor. AACR 2 directs (rule 21.7) that such works should be entered under title. Title entry is also to be chosen, according to this rule, for collections of independent works by different persons or bodies, or collections of extracts from such works. In either case, if there is no *collective* title, then entry is made under the heading appropriate to the first work or contribution (21.7C).

Study rule 21.7 and choose a main entry heading for each of the following items:

a)

GREAT BRITAIN:
GEOGRAPHICAL ESSAYS

Edited by
Jean Mitchell

Each chapter is written by an expert in a particular field.

b)

STUDIES IN COST ANALYSIS

Edited by
David Solomons

The editor states in his preface: 'I have tried to bring together some of the best work done in the field of industrial accounting during the last twenty years'.

c)

AN ANTHOLOGY OF MODERN ANIMAL WRITING

Edited by Frances Pitt

This item consists of samples from the work of twenty to thirty writers.

d)

PILGRIM'S PROGRESS

THE DREAM OF GERONTIUS

PRACTICE OF THE PRESENCE OF GOD

This collection of works, by John Bunyan, Cardinal Newman and Brother Lawrence respectively, although they are not named on the title page, is part of the Bagster's Christian classics series.

Turn to frame 86 for the answers

FRAME 57

We have now considered basic rules for entry of:

1)	Works for which a single person or corporate body is responsible	Rule 21.4
2)	Works of unknown or uncertain authorship or by unnamed groups	Rule 21.5
3)	Works of shared responsibility	Rule 21.6
4)	Collections and works produced under editorial direction	Rule 21.7

The next few frames are designed to test and reinforce your knowledge of these rules. Remember that it may also be necessary to refer to rule 21.1.

Firstly, decide which of the above conditions of authorship relate to each of the following works:

a)
THE BOOK OF
COMMON PRAYER

AND ADMINISTRATION OF THE SACRAMENTS AND OTHER RITES AND CEREMONIES OF THE CHURCH ACCORDING TO THE USE OF THE CHURCH OF ENGLAND

b)
THE TRUMPET MAJOR

by

Thomas Hardy

Edited by

Mrs F. S. Boas

c)
CONVERSATIONS BETWEEN

THE CHURCH OF ENGLAND AND THE METHODIST CHURCH

d)
THE OXFORD BOOK OF ENGLISH VERSE, 1250-1918

Chosen and edited by
Sir Arthur Quiller-Couch

e)
RELAX

How You Can Feel Better, Reduce
Stress, and Overcome Tension

EDITED BY JOHN WHITE AND JAMES FADIMAN

The 'blurb' on the back cover of this work states that: 'a wide range of experts share their secrets for easing tension'

Turn to frame 79 for the answers

48

FRAME 58
Determine the main entry heading for each of the following items:

a)   ZINC ABSTRACTS

This is a monthly publication prepared by the Zinc Development Association / Lead Development Association Abstracting Service.

b)   CHOPIN'S GREATEST HITS

In this album of sound recordings, a noted French pianist and two internationally famous conductors interpret the music of one of the greatest masters.

c)   THE FIGHTING TEMERAIRE

A painting by J.M.W. Turner.

Turn to frame 82 for the answers

FRAME 59
We have seen that, when considering the conditions of authorship relating to a particular work, one of the first questions to be asked is whether single authorship, shared authorship, or authorship of mixed character is involved.

A work of mixed responsibility, which has already been mentioned in frame 52, is one where different persons or bodies have contributed to its intellectual or artistic content by performing different kinds of activity, eg the person or body responsible for the original and a reviser, or the person or body responsible for the text and an illustrator, etc.

Such works are dealt with in rules 21.9 to 21.27. If you look again at the contents list on page 279 of AACR 2, this will give you some idea of the sort of problems that may arise and the numbers of the relevant rules.

For example, the book *Ekorn the squirrel*: adapted for children by Ruth Orbach from *Ekorn*, by Haakon Lie, involves authorship of mixed character, ie an adapter and the original author. One of these must be chosen as the entry heading. If you consult the index to AACR 2 under 'Adaptations', you will see that the rule which will help you to choose between 'adapter or original author' is rule 21.10. The contents list on page 279 of AACR 2 will also pinpoint this same rule. If you turn to this rule, you will find that entry for the work in question will be under the adapter.

Which rule would you use to determine the entry heading for a translation?

Turn to frame 66 for the answer

FRAME 60

There are two basic categories of mixed authorship:

i)   where a previously existing work has been modified as with revisions, adaptations or translations

ii) a new work to which different persons or bodies have made different contributions, eg a collaborative work by a writer and an artist, or a work which reports an interview.

As you may have noticed, AACR 2 treats these as two separate problems. rules 21.9 to 21.23 deal with i) and rules 21.24 to 21.27 with ii).

Have a further look at the contents list on page 279 of AACR 2 to confirm this and then proceed to next frame.

FRAME 61

The general rule for the entry of works which are modifications of other works is to enter under the heading appropriate to the new work *only* if the nature and content of the original or if the medium of expression has been changed (21.9).

For example, Charles Lamb wrote his *Tales from Shakespeare* in prose rather than verse so that this constitutes a change in the medium of expression and entry would be made under the heading for Lamb. Dickens' *Oliver Twist*, retold for boys and girls by Russell Thorndike, contains only a fraction of the original work and the language is very much simplified. Entry is, therefore, again under the heading appropriate to the new work, ie the heading for Thorndike.

Examine rules 21.9 to 21.15 and then decide on the headings under which entry would be made for:

a)   MORSE THEORY

by
J. MILNOR
Based on lecture notes
by M. Spivak and R. Wells

b)   THE STORY OF DAVID COPPERFIELD

BY

CHARLES DICKENS

Abridged by

W. JEWESBURY

The back cover states that this selection of episodes from the original story is told in Charles Dickens' own words.

Turn to frame 75 for the answers

FRAME 62

Certain media have special problems with regard to 'modification' and these have been separately treated in AACR 2 (although the general rule should still be taken into account). Such media include:

Art works (rules 21.16 and 21.17)

Music (rules 21.18 to 21.22)

Sound recordings (rule 21.23)

The sort of problems that are dealt with include: adaptations of art works from one medium to another (enter under the adapter — rule 21.16); arrangements of musical works (enter under the composer — rule 21.18); sound recordings of musical or literary works (enter a sound recording of one musical or literary work under the heading appropriate to that work — rule 21.23A; enter a sound recording containing musical or literary works by different persons or bodies under the principal performer — rule 21.23C — if there are more than three performers and no principal performer, enter under title — rule 21.23D).

Examine rules 21.16 to 21.23 and then choose entry headings for the following items:

i)   A reproduction of Turner's painting *The fighting Temeraire* made by the firm Athena Reproductions.

ii)   Music from Beethoven's *Pathétique* arranged by James Last.

iii)   Frank Sinatra's *Best of ol' blue eyes*, a sound recording of songs by various composers.

Turn to frame 68 for the answers

FRAME 63

Rules 21.24 to 21.27 deal with mixed responsibility in new works, eg collaboration between artist and writer (enter under the one named first unless the other is given greater prominence—rule 21.24) and reports of interviews and exchanges (entry depends upon whether the report is confined to the words of the person reported—rule 21.25).

Using these rules decide what the main entry heading would be under for the following item:

Frederick Wilkinson

GUNS

illustrated by Michael Shoebridge

Illustrations appear upon almost every page, take up about the same amount of space as the text and are an essential feature of the work.

Turn to frame 70 for the answer

FRAME 64

A work which has a relationship to some other work, such as a supplement, an index, a concordance, a libretto, a screenplay, a special number of a serial, etc, is entered under its own heading and *not* the heading for the work to which it is related, according to the appropriate rules in Chapter 21. This provision is contained in the general rule for related works—21.28B* but it should be noted that for particular types of relationship, eg revisions, or translations, rules 21.9 to 21.27 should be used.

According to this general rule for related works, Cruden's concordance to the Bible would, for instance, be entered under Cruden.

Examine the many examples provided in rule 21.28 and then decide upon entry headings for:

---

* *As noted in the introduction to this program, types of publication such as concordances, which come within the general rule for related works, may well be found in the index to AACR 2*

a)   SPECTATOR'S CHOICE
         Articles reprinted from *The Spectator*

         Edited by George Hutchinson

b) WILLIAMS ON THE LAW AND PRACTICE RELATING TO THE

   CONTRACT FOR SALE OF LAND AND THE TITLE TO LAND

              2nd (Cumulative) Supplement
                        by
                   R.T. Oerton

Turn to frame 78 for the answers

FRAME 65
Chapter 21 includes some special rules (21.31 to 21.39) which are
concerned with certain legal and religious publications.
   Two of the more important are rules 21.31 and 21.37. The former
deals with laws and, in general, laws which govern one jurisdiction are
entered under the heading for the jurisdiction governed (rule 21.31B1);
a compilation of laws governing more than one jurisdiction is entered
as a collection.
   Rule 21.37 deals with sacred scriptures, which are entered under
title. A *uniform* title (see phase five − frame 162 −) may be used.
   Examine rules 21.31 to 21.39. Trace the rule which would apply to
a bi-partite treaty between Great Britain and the United States of
America.
   Turn to frame 84 for the answer

FRAME 66
The relevant rule is 21.14. This number could have been found by consulting the index to AACR 2 under 'Translations' or by scanning the
contents list on page 279
   Proceed to frame 60

FRAME 67

The answer is the heading for R.F. Baldwin. When there are not more than three responsible persons or bodies and a principal responsibility is not indicated, entry is under the first named.

Proceed to frame 54

FRAME 68

The appropriate entry headings are those for:

i) Turner (rule 21.16B applies)
ii) Beethoven (rule 21.18B applies)
iii) Sinatra (rule 21.23C applies)

Return to the rules noted if you were incorrect to see how these answers have been obtained, then proceed to frame 63

FRAME 69

A change occurs in the first five words of the title and this does, therefore, constitute a change in title proper according to the definition given in rule 21.2.

Proceed to frame 46

FRAME 70

Rule 21.24 is the relevant rule. Where a work is the result of collaboration between an artist and a writer, entry is under the heading for the one named first unless the other's name is given greater prominence. Entry is, therefore, in this instance, under the heading for Wilkinson, the author of the text.

Proceed to frame 64

FRAME 71

A work of unknown authorship, such as *The Christmas anthology*, is entered under title. *John Dalton and the progress of science* is also entered under title, as this is a work by an unnamed group.

The above decisions were taken in accordance with rule 21.5 but rule 21.1B1 is also relevant in the latter case. The corporate body concerned, which is a conference, is considered not to have a name because initial letters of words are not capitalised and the indefinite article is used.

Proceed to frame 52

FRAME 72

The probable headings or access points would be:

The person responsible for the work: The heading for John J. Ogle

The series: The library series

The title: The free library

Proceed to frame 43

FRAME 73

This is a collection of official papers by *one* person and it would, therefore, be entered under the personal heading (William V.S. Tubman) and not under the corporate heading for the president (rule 21.4D3). An added entry would be made under the corporate heading.

Proceed to frame 50

FRAME 74

The *Encyclopaedia of world cookery* is a work of 'single personal authorship' and this is the *condition* of authorship which should be consulted in the index to AACR 2. Note that it is totally wrong to attempt to find a rule for entering the *type* of publication and the term 'encyclopedias' does not appear in the index to the rules.

Friction materials for engineers is a work 'emanating from a single corporate body' and this is the *condition* which should be looked for in the index, ie 'Single corporate body, works emanating from'.

Proceed to frame 48

FRAME 75

Rule 21.12B is applicable to a), the wording of the title page does appear to indicate that the persons responsible for the original lecture notes are no longer responsible for the work. Entry would therefore be made under the heading for Milnor. Item b) is covered by the general rule 21.9, an abridgment being entered under the heading appropriate to the original, ie the heading for Dickens.

Proceed to frame 62

FRAME 76

The *Encyclopaedia of world cookery* would be entered under the single person responsible according to rule 21.4A. *Friction materials for engineers* is, however, a work emanating from a corporate body which does *not* fall within the categories given in rule 21.1B2. It does not, therefore, come within the compass of rule 21.4B but would be entered under title according to rule 21.1C.

Proceed to frame 49

FRAME 77

When there are more than three persons or bodies responsible and principal responsibility is not indicated, entry is under title (see rule 21.6C2).

Proceed to frame 56

FRAME 78

As we have seen, according to rule 21.28B, a related work is to be entered under its own heading according to the appropriate rule in Chapter 21. *Spectator's choice* must, therefore, be treated as a collection and would be entered under title according to the provisions of rule 21.7. Item b), the supplement, is a work of a single personal authorship and would therefore be entered under the heading for Oerton according to the provisions of rules 21.1A2 and 21.4A.

Proceed to frame 65

FRAME 79

The conditions of authorship are:

a) Single corporate authorship, ie The Church of England. Rule 21.4B applies and rule 21.1B2 is also relevant as this would be considered to be a work of an administrative nature dealing with the policies and procedures of the corporate body itself.

b) Single personal authorship (rule 21.4A). The fact that there is an editor is irrelevant in this instance; this is the work of one person, ie Hardy.

c) Shared authorship. Category (4) of rule 21.6A applies. Again, rule 21.1B2 is relevant.

d) This is a collection of extracts from independent works by different persons (rule 21.7A–category 2).
e) This is obviously a work consisting of contributions by different persons produced under editorial direction (rule 21.7A–category 3).
Proceed to frame 58

FRAME 80

The answer is the heading for Dobbins as he is the *principal* person responsible. This can be indicated by either wording or layout. In this case both are used. See rule 21.6B1.

If you were right, proceed to frame 55. If you were wrong, go over the example again and make sure that you understand it before proceeding.

FRAME 81

The main entry headings would be:
a) The heading for P.M. Soderburg
b) The heading for the British Museum
c) Street map of Formby
d) Library assistant

In the case of a), entry is made under the single person responsible for the work (rule 21.1A2) and in the case of b) under the single corporate body responsible for the work. In the latter instance, the work falls within category (a) of rule 21.1B2 as it is a catalogue describing the resources of the corporate body. The *Street map of Formby* and the serial *Library assistant* also emanate from corporate bodies but, in these cases, the items do not fall within any of the categories given in rule 21.1B2 and entry is, therefore, under title according to the provisions of rule 21.1C.

Proceed to frame 45

FRAME 82
The main entry headings would be:
a)   Zinc abstracts

     This work emanates from a corporate body but does not fall into one of the categories given in rule 21.1B2. It is therefore entered under title according to rule 21.1C. Rule 21.4B is, therefore, irrelevant in this particular instance.

b)   The heading for Chopin

c)   The heading for Turner

     In each of these instances, a single person is responsible for the intellectual or artistic content. Rules 21.1A and 21.4A apply.

This completes the short test of your knowledge of the basic rules.
Proceed to frame 59

FRAME 83
This is *shared* responsibility, which occurs when more than one person or body have a similar relationship to the work.

Proceed to frame 53

FRAME 84
The relevant rule is 21.35A1, which is concerned with international treaties between two or three national governments. It should have been reasonably easy to locate this rule as you studied the special rules for certain legal publications. An entry for 'Treaties, intergovernmental agreements, etc', with appropriate references, also appears in the index to AACR 2.

This completes our introductory study of Chapter 21 of AACR 2 except for 'added entries'. These will be dealt with in the next phase but, before proceeding, return and read frame 50 again.

FRAME 85
Yes, a new entry would be required under the new name, the Association of Assistant Librarians, according to the provisions of rule 21.3B(1).

The change of title to *Assistant librarian* would require a separate main entry according to the provisions of rule 21.2C. The change involves an alteration in the 'first five words' and it is, therefore, a 'change in title proper' as defined in rule 21.2A.

Proceed to frame 47

FRAME 86

Item i) is a work of multiple authorship produced under the direction of an editor. Items ii) and iii) consist of independent works, or extracts from such works, which have been collected together by an editor. In all three of these instances, rule 21.7 directs that main entry should be under title. Item iv), however, has no collective title and is therefore entered under the heading appropriate to the first work. This would be the heading for the single person responsible, ie that for John Bunyan.

Proceed to frame 57

PHASE THREE

CHOICE OF ACCESS POINTS
ADDED ENTRIES

AACR 2 Mentioned throughout
rules in Chapter 21 and
specifically covered in
rules 21.29 and 21.30

FRAME 87

A reader may make many approaches when searching for a particular item; the 'author' approach, the 'title' approach, the 'series' approach, etc. All of these various types of entry headings, or access points, must be considered by the indexer.

In the last phase, we were primarily concerned with the choice of main entry headings, although, as was noted in frame 50, Chapter 21 also indicates the added entries that are required in the particular circumstances with which each rule deals. For example, rule 21.12A tells us to make an added entry under the name of the reviser when main entry is under the original author. In addition to instructions in specific rules, the general principles which should be taken into account when making added entries are stated in rules 21.29 and 21.30.

An examination of rule 21.29 will indicate that, in general, an entry may be made under any heading that could be important for retrieval purposes.

Rule 21.30 deals more specifically with the added entries to be made under collaborating authors, titles, series, etc.

Now try this problem. If a work has four personal authors, none of whom is represented as principal author, then main entry is under title. Would any added entries be necessary for the authors? In making your decision, refer both to the specific rule for works of shared responsibility and to rule 21.30.

Turn to frame 96 for the answer.

FRAME 88

Rule 21.14 directs that an added entry be made under the heading for a translator if appropriate under the provisions of 21.30K1. Examine these two rules and decide whether an added entry would be necessary for Leonard Tancock as translator of Zola's *Thérèse Raquin* into English. This work has also been translated into English by various other people.

Turn to frame 98 for the answer.

FRAME 89

Find the appropriate rule number for added title entries. Would an added title entry be necessary for each of the following items?

a) Rodin's sculpture *The kiss*
b) the sound recording entitled *Francis Albert Sinatra and Antonio Carlos Jobim*, songs and music by various composers
c) *Coins*, a printed monograph by John Porteous

Turn to frame 95 for the answer.

FRAME 90

Find the appropriate rule for series added entries. Would an added entry be necessary for either of the following series?

a) British Parliamentary papers
b) Living Shakespeare—a series of sound recordings of Shakespeare's plays.

Turn to frame 99 for the answer.

FRAME 91

Main entry for the following work would be under Daniell. Would added entries be necessary for:

(a) the illustrator
(b) the title
(c) the series

YOUR BODY

by DAVID SCOTT DANIELL
with illustrations by ROBERT AYTON

This is one of the *Ladybird book series*, published by Wills and Hepworth, of which there are hundreds of titles covering a wide range of subjects and reading ages. The books have a similar physical format.

The illustrator is given the same prominence as the author and the illustrations are an important feature of the work.

Turn to frame 97 for the answer.

FRAME 92

Return to the Oerton example used in frame 64. Would an added entry be required for the work to which this supplement is related?

Turn to frame 100 for the answer.

FRAME 93

Return to the example *Modern mathematics at Ordinary Level* used in frame 8 and for which possible access points were considered in frame 42. Which of these access points must be chosen as the main entry heading and would added entries be necessary for the remainder?

Turn to frame 94 for the answer

FRAME 94

The main entry heading would be the heading for Clarke, as this is the single personal author primarily responsible for the content of the work (rules 21.1A2 and 21.4A). Added entries would be needed under the title (according to rule 21.30J) and under the series (according to rule 21.30L).

You should now know enough about AACR 2's treatment of added entries to be able to apply the relevant rules. Remember that, when in doubt about the interpretation of a particular rule, it is better to make an added entry rather than not make one. Remember also that the rules provide guidelines only. It is possible, as indicated in frame 87, to make an added entry for any possible access point that you think may be 'sought'.

One last point to be noted is that some catalogues are based upon the principle of *alternative headings*; the various headings required are simply added above the standard description and no attempt is made to distinguish between main and added entries. For such catalogues, Chapter 21 can still be used as a guide to the headings that should be selected as access points (see General introduction to AACR 2 section 0.5).

Proceed to phase 4, following frame 100.

FRAME 95

Rule 21.30J is the appropriate rule number for added title entries. An added title entry would be necessary for a) *The kiss*. In the case of b), however, the main entry heading would be the heading for Sinatra and an added entry would be necessary for the performer who shares responsibility, Jobim. It seems likely therefore, that an added entry under title would be superfluous. This is borne out by rule 21.30J(1), which directs that an added entry under title is not necessary when the title proper is essentially the same as the main entry heading.

Where c) is concerned, an added title entry would be made *unless* the catalogue is one in which author/title and subject entries are interfiled. The title entry would, in the latter instance, in all probability be the same as the subject heading used for the work which would make a title entry unnecessary.

Proceed to frame 90

FRAME 96
The relevant rule for works of shared responsibility is 21.6C2. This directs that an added entry must be made under the heading for the first person named. Rule 21.30B also contains this same instruction.

Proceed to frame 88

FRAME 97
The choice of the heading for Daniell as the heading for the main entry for this work is made in accordance with rule 21.11, that is under the heading appropriate to the text. This rule directs that an added entry should be made under the heading for the illustrator if appropriate under the provisions of 21.30K. After referring to rule 21.30K2, it becomes clear that an added entry for the illustrator would be necessary because his name is given 'equal prominence' and the illustrations are considered to be an important feature of the work. A title entry would also be required according to the provisions of rule 21.30J. A series entry would not, however, be necessary because, in the words of rule 21.30L, 'the items in the series are related to each other only by common physical characteristics'.*

Proceed to frame 92

---

* *Students conversant with this series will know that 'Ladybird books' is now the publisher.*

FRAME 98
An added entry under the translator would be necessary because the work has been translated into the same language more than once (rule 21.30K1(c) applies).
   Proceed to frame 89

FRAME 99
The appropriate rule number for series added entries is 21.30L. In the case of British Parliamentary papers and Living Shakespeare, a series entry would seem to provide a useful collocation according to the wording of this rule and they would, therefore, be necessary.
   Proceed to frame 91

FRAME 100
Yes, an added entry would be required for the work to which the Oerton supplement is related. (Rule 21.30G applies).
   Proceed to frame 93

PHASE FOUR

HEADINGS

FRAME 101

Having chosen the access points, or headings, under which a particular item is to be entered in the catalogue, problems may still be encountered with regard to *how* such headings are to be entered. For example, if, using Chapter 21, it is decided that an entry is to be made under the name Foo Kwac Wah, which part of the name will come first in the heading? Obviously we need some direction.

Headings for *persons* are dealt with in Chapter 22.

Headings for *geographic names* are dealt with in Chapter 23.

Headings for *corporate bodies* are dealt with in Chapter 24.

Proceed to next frame

FRAME 102

In chapter 22, there are basically two problems involved:

i)   Concerns the choice between the different names or different forms of name by which a person might be known, eg a real name and a pseudonym, or names in more than one language, etc.

ii) Concerns the way in which the chosen name is to be entered; it may be confusing or unfamiliar, eg names with prefixes, compound names, foreign names, etc, and guidance may be required as to which part to select as the entry element.

In accordance with the general structure of AACR 2, the first basic rule of Chapter 22 is prepotent. This is rule 22.1, which states that a person is entered under the name by which he or she is *commonly known.* This is most important and thus we would choose, as a basis for headings, names such as:

Jimmy Carter *not* James Earl Carter

Duke Ellington *not* Edward Kennedy Ellington

The following names would not be those chosen for the people concerned because they are better known by other names. Do you know what these other names are?

Frederick Austerlitz

Norma Jean Baker

William Claude Dukinfield

Angelo Siciliano

Turn to frame 118 for the answer

FRAME 103

Read through rule 22.1 and choose the form of heading that you would use for the author H.G. Wells:

Herbert George Wells

or H   G   Wells

or H.G. Wells

Turn to frame 125 for the answer

FRAME 104

The rules following the prepotent rule, 22.1, deal more specifically with the two basic problems indicated in frame 102. The first of these problems is that of a person known by different names (see rule 22.2) or different forms of the same name (see rule 22.3). Note that these rules conform with the basic rule in that, if one name or form of name predominates and is clearly the name by which a person is most commonly known, then this is the name under which entry is made. Otherwise, one name or form of name is chosen according to the order of preference shown in rule 22.2A, ie:

i)   Name appearing most frequently in the person's works.

ii)   Name appearing most frequently in reference sources.

iii)   Latest name.

Examples of persons known by different names are the comedian and author Terence Alan Milligan, alias Spike Milligan, and the tennis player R.A. Gonzales, alias 'Pancho' Gonzales. Which form of these names would you choose as a basis for entry headings?

Turn to frame 130 for the answer

FRAME 105

A common example of a person using different names is that of an author, performer, etc who adopts a pseudonym or pseudonyms for all or some of his work or performances. The relevant rule is 22.2C and this again conforms to the basic rule in that, if a person always uses the one pseudonym, entry is under that pseudonym. If a person uses several pseudonyms (or a real name and one or more pseudonyms) entry is under the predominant name if there is one. If there is no predominant name, each item is entered according to the name appearing in it.

The entertainer Jeanne Bourgeois, known as Mistinguett, is probably the most famous star in the history of the French music hall. Which name, Bourgeois or Mistinguett, would you choose as the basis of a heading for this person when entering her autobiography:

MISTINGUETT

QUEEN OF THE PARIS NIGHT

Turn to frame 128 for the answer

FRAME 106

A person may change his or her name and rule 22.2B directs that entry should be under the latest form of name unless there is reason to believe that an earlier name will persist as the name by which a person is better known.

What would you enter the author Mrs Mary Smith *née* Evans under?

Turn to frame 126 for the answer

FRAME 107

The problem of different forms of name is also evident where a title of nobility is concerned. A nobleman may be entered under his title or his family name, depending upon which form is most commonly used. As the example included in rule 22.1A shows, the Duke of Wellington would be entered under his better known title and not under his family name.

However, the acquisition of a title of nobility can involve a *change* of name, in which case rule 22.2B also applies. It may well be that the earlier family name continues to be the better known as in the example:

Benjamin Disraeli

not

Earl of Beaconsfield

A further example of names in different forms is that of those names which may be cited in two or more different languages (see rule 22.3B). Again, note how this rule tends to follow the basic rule. Entry is, therefore, made under the form of name most commonly used or most commonly found in reference sources of the person's country of residence or activity, eg:

George Mikes

not

György Mikes

Proceed to next frame

FRAME 108

Having briefly examined the problem of different names or different forms of name, let us now look at the second major problem relating to headings for persons, that is the selection of the entry element. The general rule (22.4A) states that the entry element should be that part of the name under which the person is listed in authoritative alphabetic lists in his or her own language or country, unless the person's preference is known to be different, in which case the preference is followed.

If the entry element is the first element of the name, then the name is entered in direct order (rule 22.4B1), eg:

Ram Gopal

If the first element of the name is a surname, it is followed by a comma (rule 22.4B2), eg:

Chiang, Kai-shek

If the entry element is not the first element of the name, the elements are transposed and a comma used to precede the transposition (rule 22.4B3), eg:

Smith, John

The latter would be the most usual form for names in English, ie

Surname, Forename(s)

With a few exceptions (eg entry under a title of nobility), any name that contains a surname is entered under than surname (rule 22.5A). Note, however, that a surname is not used in some cultures and, in others, it might be the *first* element, as indicated in the examples above.

Read through rules 22.4 and 22.5A. How would the following names, which have already been mentioned in previous frames, be entered in a catalogue?

> Fred Astaire
> Duke Ellington
> H.G. Wells
> Marilyn Monroe

Turn to frame 122 for the answers

FRAME 109

Many surnames do not simply consist of one name, eg 'Smith', but of more than one name, eg 'Kaye-Smith'. The latter is known as a hyphenated surname and it is a common example of what are referred to as 'compound surnames'. The question is, of course, whether a hyphenated surname should be entered under the first or second element.

Which rule of AACR 2 deals with the problem of hyphenated surnames and what form of heading would you choose for the name A.M. Carr-Saunders?

Turn to frame 121 for the answer

FRAME 110

Many compound surnames cause confusion because they have separately written prefixes. How such names are entered usually depends upon the language, or language group, to which the author's works or his name belong (rule 22.5D).

For example, in English, entry is under the prefix, eg:

De la Roche, Mazo
Le Mesurier, John
Von Braun, Wernher

(NB. The latter author's works are written in English).

Now choose the forms of heading to be used for the Dutch author Michel van der Plas and the Dutch painter Vincent van Gogh.

Turn to frame 129 for the answer

FRAME 111

It has been noted that the general rule for compound surnames (22.5C2) directs that entry should be under the element by which the person prefers to be entered or, if this is unknown, under the element under which the name is listed in reference sources in the person's language or country of residence.

What form of heading would you therefore choose for the British composer Ralph Vaughan Williams?

Turn to frame 119 for the answer

FRAME 112

Occasionally, the nature of a surname may be uncertain. Examine, in general, the rule for compound surnames (22.5C) and attempt to discover whilst doing this, whether the rule covers such an extingency. What form of heading would you use for the author Angus McTavish Brown?

Turn to frame 120 for the answer

FRAME 113

As previously indicated, a nobleman may be entered under his title or his family name. Rule 22.6 directs that entry is under the title of nobility when a person uses his or her title rather than a surname in his or her works or when such a person is listed by title in reference sources. The title is followed by the personal name in direct order and by the term of rank in the vernacular, eg:

Wellington, Arthur Wellesley, *Duke of*

When entry is not under title of nobility, the title is added to the name only if the title appears with the name in the person's works or in reference sources (see rule 22.12A), eg:

Hill, Charles, *Baron Hill of Luton*
but
Campbell, Patrick

Patrick Campbell does not use his title, Baron Glenavy, in his works; Charles Hill, in his *Memoirs* . . . does in fact do so.

Examine rules 22.6 and 22.12A. Look also at rule 22.12B which instructs that British titles of honour such as 'Sir' and 'Lady' are to be given in the heading if such a term appears with the name in works by the person or in reference sources, eg:

Beecham, *Sir* **Thomas**

You should note that rule 22.15C provides for the omission of most other titles associated with names entered under surname unless they are required to distinguish between two persons with the same name. Cardinal John Henry Newman would, therefore, be entered as:

Newman, John Henry

Upon the title page of an item appears: 'edited by Admiral Sir Reginald H.S. Bacon.' What would be the form of heading that you would choose for this person?

Turn to frame 124 for the answer

FRAME 114

When a person's name does not include a surname, entry may be made under the person's given name, etc, according to the provisions of rule 22.8. Entry is under that part of name under which the person is listed in reference sources and included in the name are any words or phrases denoting the place of origin, domicile, occupation, or other characteristic which are commonly associated with the name. Thus headings such as the following are obtained:

John, *the Baptist*
Elizabeth II, *Queen of the United Kingdom*
Francis, *of Assisi, Saint*
Pius XII, *Pope*

Additions, such as Roman numerals, titles, or other characteristics are made in accordance with rule 22.8 or rules 22.13 to 22.17 ('Additions to names').

Rules 22.9, 22.10 and 22.11, which also deal with names which do not include a surname, cover, respectively, entry of Roman names under the part most commonly used, eg:

Cicero, Marcus Tullius

entry under initials in direct order, eg:

H.D. *not* **D., H.**

and entry under a phrase, eg:

Father Time

Examine rule 22.8 and also rules 22.13 to 22.17 and formulate a heading for Saint Hilary of Poitiers, the latter name being his place of birth.

Turn to frame 127 for the answer

FRAME 115

When certain persons have the *same* name, we must be able to distinguish between them. This is done by adding dates or distinguishing terms, eg:

Jones, William, 1815-1871
Jones, William, 1897-1954
Brown, George, *Captain*
Brown, George, *Rev.*

The relevant rules are 22.18 and 22.19 It will be seen from an examination of the former rule that, *optionally*, dates may, in fact, be added to other personal names if desired.

If neither dates nor distinguishing terms are available, the same heading has to be used for all persons with the same name (rule 22.20).

You are required to distinguish between two authors, both of whom are named John Williams. All that you can discover is that one was born in 1837 and that the other died in 1959. What forms of heading would you use for these authors?

Turn to frame 117 for the answer

FRAME 116

Foreign names may be unfamiliar and rules 22.21 onwards (not forgetting preceding rules which must also be considered) provide guidance upon the treatment of names in certain languages.

A person with an Indonesian name, for example, is usually entered under the last element (rule 22.26), eg:

Hatta, Mohammad

What form of heading would be used for the contemporary Indic author's name Sarvepalli Radhakrishnan?

Turn to frame 123 for the answer

FRAME 117

The headings would be:

Williams, John, *b.* 1837

Williams, John, *d.* 1959

If you were not correct re-examine the examples given in rule 22.18.

Note that, if part of a name is represented by initials and it becomes necessary to distinguish between names which are identical, the full form may be given in parentheses (rule 22.16A), eg:

Jones, S.J. (Simon John)

Jones, S.J. (Stanley James)

Optionally, dates may be added to all personal names, even if there is no need to distinguish between headings (rule 22.18) and where names containing initials are concerned, optionally the spelled out form may always be added in parentheses.

Proceed to frame 116

FRAME 118

Frederick Austerlitz is better known as Fred Astaire;

Norma Jean Baker as Marilyn Monroe;

William Claude Dukinfield as W C Fields;

Angelo Siciliano as Charles Atlas.

Did you know all of these? Probably not, which illustrates the reasoning behind entry being made under the name by which a person is commonly known. Rule 22.1 directs that entry for each of the above would be made under the better known name.

Proceed to frame 103

FRAME 119

In British alphabetical lists, this composer is entered as:

Vaughan Williams, Ralph

and this is the form of heading which should be chosen.

Proceed to frame 112

FRAME 120

Rule 22.5C6 is the relevant section of rule 22.5C which must be used when the nature of a surname is uncertain. If the person's language is English, entry is under the last part of the name, ie

Brown, Angus McTavish

Proceed to frame 113

FRAME 121

Rule 22.5C3 instructs that entry is to be under the first element of a hyphenated surname, ie:

Carr-Saunders, A.M.

You should have had no difficulty finding this rule and answering the question. 'Hyphenated personal names—surnames' appears in the index to AACR 2 and pinpoints the relevant rule which, when consulted, is quite straightforward.

Proceed to frame 110

FRAME 122

The answers are:

    Astaire, Fred
    Ellington, Duke
    Monroe, Marilyn
    Wells, H.G.

In each of these instances, the entry element is not the first element and the elements are therefore transposed, the entry element being followed by a comma (rule 22.4B3).

Proceed to frame 109

FRAME 123

According to rule 22.25B, modern Indic names are entered under surname if known, otherwise under the last name. The answer is, therefore:

Radhakrishnan, Sarvepalli

Proceed to frame 131

FRAME 124

The heading would be:

Bacon, *Sir* **Reginald H.S.**

'Admiral' is omitted in accordance with rule 22.15C and 'Sir' is included, but italicised, in accordance with rule 22.12B.

Proceed to frame 114

FRAME 125

H.G. Wells

is the correct answer, as this is the form of name by which this author is commonly identified. Herbert George Wells is not the form of name by which Wells is usually referred to. With regard to the form H G Wells, a decision should be made in the first instance whether to use forenames in full. Spaces should not be left for completion at a later date.

Proceed to frame 104

FRAME 126

The answer is the latest name (rule 22.2B), ie:

Mary Smith

Proceed to frame 107

FRAME 127

The heading should be:

Hilary, *of Poitiers, Saint*

The rules used are numbers 22.8A and 22.13A.

Proceed to frame 115

FRAME 128

The answer is:

Mistinguett

This is the pseudonym that this performer always used and it is also the way in which she is identified in reference sources. Entry is, therefore, made under the pseudonym (rule 22.2C).

Proceed to frame 106

FRAME 129

Rule 22.5D1 *Dutch* directs that entry is to be made under the part following the prefix unless the prefix is 'ver'. According to this rule, entry would, therefore, be under:

Plas, Michel van der

and

Gogh, Vincent van

However, note should be taken of the general rule 22.5C2 which states that a compound surname is entered under the element by which the person bearing the name prefers to be entered or, if this is unknown, under the element under which it is listed in reference sources. Probably entry would be better made, therefore, under:

Van Gogh, Vincent

where the latter name is concerned.

Proceed to frame 111

FRAME 130

Spike Milligan

and

Pancho Gonzales

are the names which should be chosen as the basis for entry headings. These are the names by which these persons are commonly known and also the forms in which the names appear in works written by Milligan, in Gonzales' autobiography *Man with a racket* and in reference sources.

Proceed to frame 105

FRAME 131

Chapter 23 of AACR 2 deals with 'Geographic names', the 'places' which frequently constitute essential elements in headings for corporate bodies. They may be required to differentiate bodies with identical names; they may be used as additions to corporate names (eg for conferences); and, in many instances, they are used as headings for governments.

The English form of name, as determined from gazetteers or other reference sources, is the one to be used whenever possible (rule 23.2A), eg:

Austria
not
Österreich

If there is no English form in general use, prefer the form in the official language of the country (rule 23.2B).

If it is necessary to differentiate between two places of the same name, the name of the larger geographical entity in which the place is located is added in parentheses (rule 23.4), eg:

Bangor (*Gwynedd*)
Bangor (*Northern Ireland*)

If a geographic name begins with a term indicating a type of political jurisdiction, enter under the element most frequently found as the entry element in lists published in the language of the country in which the place is located (rule 23.5), eg:

Kerry (*Ireland*) *not* **County Kerry** (*Ireland*)
but
District of Columbia (*U.S.*)

How would these rules help you to distinguish between the English County Borough of Bootle, Lancashire, and the English parish of Bootle in Cumberland? Both of these places ceased to exist as local government authorities in 1974, when Bootle, Lancashire, became part of the Metropolitan District of Sefton and Bootle Cumberland, was absorbed by the County of Cumbria.

Turn to frame 132 for the answer

FRAME 132

The answer is:

Bootle (*Cumberland*)
Bootle (*Lancashire*)

Rule 23.4D3 directs that if the heading is for a place which ceased to exist in 1974, the name of the geographical county in which the place was located at the time of cessation is to be added for differentiation purposes.

Proceed to next frame

FRAME 133

Chapter 24 of AACR 2 deals with headings for corporate bodies. The basic prepotent rule in this chapter states that, in general, entry is made under the *name* of the body as determined from items issued by the body in its language (rule 24.1), eg:

Alder Hey Children's Hospital
Aslib
Association of Consulting Engineers
Breitkopf & Härtel
Conservative and Unionist Party
Ecole centrale lyonnaise
National Science Foundation
Scottish Genealogy Society
Unesco
University of Liverpool
Yale University

The only exceptions are:

i)   Subordinate bodies which may need to be entered under a higher body, eg:

Stanford University. *Department of Civil Engineering*

ii) A body which may need to be entered under the name of a government, eg:

United States. *Department of Commerce*

Now decide upon the headings to be used for the British Goat Society and the United States Capitol Historical Society.

Turn to frame 161 for the answer.

FRAME 134

When the name of a body changes, a new heading is established for publications appearing under the new name. This means that various items by the one body may appear under different headings, eg:

> **United Kingdom.** *Board of Trade. Labour Department*

and

> **United Kingdom.** *Ministry of Labour*

and

> **United Kingdom.** *Department of Employment and Productivity*

In 1969, a pamphlet was issued by the Ministry of Transport of the United Kingdom.

In October, 1970, the Ministry of Transport was amalgamated with other ministries to form the new Department of the Environment.

In 1971, you have to catalogue the pamphlet issued in 1969. What form of heading would you choose?

> **United Kingdom.** *Ministry of Transport*

or

> **United Kingdom.** *Department of the Environment*

Turn to frame 154 for the answer

FRAME 135

One of the many problems connected with headings for corporate bodies is that of variant name forms (see rules 24.2 and 24.3), eg:

> N.A.S.A.

and

> National Aeronautics and Space Administration

> Canadian Library Association

and

> Association canadienne des bibliothèques

Usually, in agreement with the general rule which was considered in frame 133, the form to be used is that given in the item with which the body is concerned and in its official language.

If, however, variant forms of name are found in items issued by a body, then the name should be used as it appears in the 'chief source of information' (rule 24.2B).

If variant forms appear in the chief source of information, then the form to be used is that which is presented formally.

If no form is presented formally, then the predominant form is to be used.

If there is no predominant form, then rule 24.2D lays down an 'order of precedence': 1 Brief form (if there is one); 2 Form found in reference sources; 3 Official form.

Examine rule 24.2 and answer the following questions:

a)   On the title page of a serial appears:

Ladsirlac Information Bulletin

Ladsirlac is an acronym for the Liverpool and District Scientific, Industrial and Research Library Advisory Council. What form of heading would you choose for this body?

b)   A publication is issued by the National Railroad Passenger Corporation of America, ie Amtrak. The latter form of name is given greater prominence on the title page. Which is the form of name that you would adopt for an entry heading?

Turn to frame 157 for the answers

FRAME 136

Rule 24.3 contains further special instructions for variant names of corporate bodies.

Rules 24.3A and 24.3B are concerned with names in different languages. The form in the official language is to be preferred, or, if there is more than one official language, one of which is English, the English form is to be preferred. If English is not one of the official languages or if the official language is not known, then the form to be selected is the form in the language predominantly used in items issued by the body. If the name of an international body appears in English on items issued by it, then this English form is to be used. In cases of doubt, the order of preference for forms in various languages is English, French, German, Spanish, Russian.

Rules 24.3C to 24.3G cover some special instances of variant names which may occur in the case of ancient bodies, international bodies, religious orders, governments, etc. The general rule (24.3C1) is to prefer the conventional name where there is one, eg:

Westminster Abbey *not* Collegiate Church of St. Peter in Westminster

The conventional name of the country, county, state, city, borough, municipality, etc. is usually used as a heading for its government (rule

24.3E). Note that the conventional *English* form of name is preferred (see also frame 131), eg:

France *not* République française

Examine this rule. What would be the heading for a work issued in Britain by Her Majesty's Government?

Turn to frame 149 for the answer

FRAME 137

Rules 24.4 and 24.5 deal with additions and modifications to names. Important general instances when *additions* are necessary include:

i)   When the name does not convey the idea of a corporate body (rule 24.4B); a general designation is added, eg:

Apollo (*Spacecraft*)

Racing Cars (*Musical group*)

ii)   When two or more bodies have the same name (rule 24.4C); one of the following is added to distinguish between them:

The name of the place in which the body is located, eg:

Loyola University (*Chicago*)

Loyola University (*New Orleans*)

The name of the institution of which the body is part, eg:

Newman Club (*Brooklyn College*)

Newman Club (*University of Maryland*)

The year of founding, eg:

Scientific Society of San Antonio (*1892-1894*)

Scientific Society of San Antonio (*1904-   *)

If the place, name of institution, or date is insufficient, then some other appropriate designation may be added, eg:

Church of God (*Adventist*)

Church of God (*Apostolic*)

Important general instances of *omissions* are:

i)   Initial articles unless required for reasons of grammar Rule 24.5A), eg:

Library Association

not The Library Association

ii)   Terms indicating incorporation and certain other terms such as 'Limited', unless they are integral parts of a name or they are needed to make clear that the name is that of a corporate body (rule 24.5C), eg:

American Ethnological Society *without* 'Inc.'

Examine rules 24.4 and 24.5 and formulate headings for the group The Drifters, for the firm Cecil E. Watts Limited and for Philadelphia '76, Inc., the bicentennial agency of the City of Philadelphia.

Turn to frame 151 for the answers

FRAME 138

The special rules 24.6 to 24.11 deal with additions and modifications to names of governments, conferences, exhibitions, chapters, local churches and radio and television stations.

Rule 24.6 is applicable only to governments with the same conventional name that remain undifferentiated by previous rules. For example, for governments other than those of cities and towns, the type of jurisdiction may be added, eg:

Guadalajaru (*Spain*)
Guadalajaru (*Spain : Province*)

An important rule in this section is that for conferences (24.7). The name of a conference is followed by the number, date and location, which may be the name of an institution, given in parentheses, eg:

Conference on the Pathobiology of Trauma (*1973 : University of Minnesota*)
Louisiana Cancer Conference (*2nd : 1958 : New Orleans*)

Study rules 24.6 and 24.7. Formulate a heading for the First National Conference on Childminding held at Bradford in 1975.

Turn to frame 148 for the answer

FRAME 139

Now examine rules 24.8 to 24.11 and choose a heading for the Washington Memorial Chapel, which is situated in Valley Forge, Pennsylvania. Make any necessary additions to the chosen form of heading.

Turn to frame 153 for the answer

FRAME 140

One of the two exceptions to entry of a corporate body directly under its name occurs when a subordinate body is entered under a higher body of which it is part or to which it is related.

In rule 24.13 will be found listed five types of body which must be entered in this way. The procedure is to see whether a subordinate or related body fits into one of these types. If it does, then it must be entered as a subheading, eg:

.   **Library Association.** *Cataloguing and Indexing Group*

If it does not, then it is entered under its own name according to the general rules.

Examine rules 24.12 and 24.13 and decide upon the forms of heading to be used for:

a)   the Museum which is part of the Royal College of Surgeons
b)   the Graduate School of Library Science of Drexel University
c) i   the Statistical Office of the United Nations
   ii the International Labour Organisation, which is also part of the United Nations

Turn to frame 156 for the answers

FRAME 141

Note that it may be necessary to use more than one rule when deciding upon forms of heading. Note also that conferences may be treated as subordinate bodies. Bearing these points in mind, what would be the forms of heading to be used for the Distributor Sales Division of Mullard Limited and for the first Annual Conference of the Association of Child Care Officers held at Manchester?

Turn to frame 159 for the answers

FRAME 142

Rule 24.14 gives instruction for entering subordinate bodies belonging to the types listed in the preceding rule (24.13). This rule is particularly relevant when there are more than two elements in an 'hierarchy'. Is, for instance, the Cataloging and Classification Section of the Resources and Technical Services Division of the American Library Association to be entered as:

American Library Association. *Resources and Technical Services Division. Cataloging and Classification Section*

or

American Library Association. *Cataloging and Classification Section*

The example in rule 24.4 indicates that the latter is the correct form of entry, the rule being that the subordinate body is to be entered as a subheading of the lowest element in the hierarchy that can be

88

entered under its own name. Any intervening elements can be omitted unless the name of the subordinate body has been, or is likely to be, used by another body entered under the same higher body.

What form of heading would you use for the Department of Library and Information Studies which is part of the Faculty of Humanities and Social Studies of Liverpool Polytechnic?

Turn to frame 150 for the answer

FRAME 143

Rules 24.15 and 24.16 are concerned with two specific types of subordinate or related bodies, namely 'joint committees' and 'state and local elements of American political parties'. Read through these rules, noting how rule 24.15A, in effect, simply repeats the basic rule for entry directly under the name of the body, and then proceed to next frame.

FRAME 144

The second exception to entry of a corporate body directly under name occurs when a government body is entered as a subheading under the name of the government.

A procedure similar to that explained in frame 140 is followed in that, if a body created or controlled by a government fits into one of the ten types listed in rule 24.18, then it must be entered as a subheading, eg:

United States. *Commission on Civil Rights*

If the body does not fit into one of the types, then it is entered directly under its own name.

Study rules 24.17 and 24.18 and decide upon the form of heading that you would use for the British Library.

Turn to frame 155 for the answer

FRAME 145

Continuing our study of rules 24.17 and 24.18, attempt to formulate headings for Liverpool City Libraries and for the Council which controls local government in Liverpool.

Turn to frame 158 for the answers

FRAME 146

Rules 24.20 to 24.26 are concerned with a variety of bodies which are connected with government, eg government officials, legislative bodies, constitutional conventions, courts, armed forces, embassies and delegations.

As an example, the heading for a chief of state, in his or her official capacity, would take the form:

>**United States.** *President (1953-1961 : Eisenhower)*

or, for a head of government, the form:

>**United Kingdom.** *Prime Minister*

The heading for any other government official is that of the ministry or agency which he represents, eg:

>**United States.** *General Accounting Office*
>*not* United States. *Comptroller General*

Examine these rules and then choose the form of heading to be used for the Grenadier Guards, which ranks first in order of precedence among infantry regiments of the British Army.

Turn to frame 152 for the answer

FRAME 147

The last rule in this chapter, rule 24.27 deals with religious bodies and officials. Examine this rule and then formulate headings for the Diocese of York of the Church of England and the Archdiocese of Washington of the Roman Catholic Church.

Turn to frame 160 for the answer

FRAME 148

The answer is:

>**National Conference on Childminding** *(lst : 1975 : Bradford)*

If you did not get this correct answer, read through rule 24.7 again, noting how the heading is derived. In particular, note the transposition of the number (rules 24.7A and 24.7B).

Proceed to frame 139

FRAME 149

The conventional name (see rule 24.3E) for the United Kingdom of Great Britain and Northern Ireland is:

United Kingdom

and this is the form of heading which should be used for Her Majesty's Government.

This should have become apparent from the examples included in previous frames (eg frame 134) and also from chapter 23.

Proceed to frame 137

FRAME 150

The answer is:

> **Liverpool Polytechnic.** *Department of Library and Information Studies*

Liverpool Polytechnic is entered directly under its name according to the basic rule 24.1. The department comes within rule 24.13 Type 4 and must, therefore, be entered as a subheading under the higher body. The intervening element in the hierarchy, Faculty of Humanities and Social Studies, is omitted under the provisions of rule 24.14.

Proceed to frame 143

FRAME 151

The answers are:

> **Drifters** (*Musical group*)

Note the addition of a designation to indicate that this is a corporate body (rule 24.4B) and the omission of the initial article (rule 24.5A);

> **Cecil E. Watts Limited**

Entry is directly under name without modification and 'limited' is needed to show that the name is that of a corporate body (rule 24.5C1).

> **Philadelphia '76, Inc.**

Again, 'Inc' is needed to show that the name is that of a corporate body.

Proceed to frame 138

FRAME 152

The answer is:

United Kingdom. *Army. Grenadier Guards*

See rules 24.18 Type 7 and rule 24.24A.

Proceed to frame 147

FRAME 153

The answer is:

Washington Memorial Chapel (*Valley Forge*)

A local church is entered according to the provisions of the basic rule (24.1) and entry, in this case, will be directly under the name. The place of location should be added in parentheses (rule 24.10B).

Proceed to frame 140

FRAME 154

Works should be entered according to the name used at the time of publication (see rule 24.1B). The answer is, therefore

United Kingdom. *Ministry of Transport*

Proceed to frame 135

FRAME 155

The answer is:

British Library

This government body does not fit into any of the types listed in rule 24.18 and it is, therefore, entered under its own name.

Proceed to frame 145

FRAME 156

The correct answers are:

a) **Royal College of Surgeons.** Museum

'Museum' is a name that is likely to be used by another higher body for one of its subordinate bodies (rule 24.13 Type 3).

b) **Drexel University.** *Graduate School of Library Science*

The name of a university faculty, school, etc., that simply indicates a particular field of study must also be entered as a subheading (rule 24.13 Type 4)

c) i **United Nations.** *Statistical Office*
   ii **International Labour Organisation**

Note the difference here. The former body comes within the scope of rule 24.13 Type 3 but the latter body does not fit into any of the types listed in rule 24.13 and it is therefore entered under its own name and not as a subheading under United Nations.

Proceed to frame 141

FRAME 157
The first answer is:
   Ladsirlac
The form of name is determined from the item issued by the body (rule 24.1—the basic rule).

If the full form of the name (Liverpool and District Scientific, Industrial and Research Library Advisory Council) also appears in the item, the answer is still Ladsirlac as this is the form which appears in the 'chief source of information', ie the title page (rules 24.2B and 12.0B1).

The second answer is
   Amtrak
If variant forms of name appear in the chief source of information (ie the title page in the case of a printed monograph—rule 2.0B1), the predominant form is to be used (rule 24.2D). If neither form predominated then Amtrak would still be the answer, as the brief form is the preferred choice in such an instance (rule 24.2D).

Proceed to frame 136

FRAME 158
The answers are:
   Liverpool City Libraries
and
   Liverpool. *Council*
The former is a body which must be entered under its own name. Despite being a government body controlled by the Liverpool local authority, it does not fit into any of the types listed in rule 24.18.

The latter is a legislative body as included in Type 5 of rule 24.18.

It may be necessary to distinguish between two or more places with the same name (see rule 23.4), in which case the last of the above headings would become:

Liverpool *(Merseyside). Council*

Proceed to frame 146

FRAME 159

The answers are:

Mullard Limited. *Distributor Sales Division*

More than one rule must be applied in this instance, rule 24.5C (see frame 137), which directs that 'Limited' may be needed to indicate that the name is that of a corporate body, and rule 24.13 Type 1, which includes 'division' as a term which implies that the body is part of another higher body.

Association of Child Care Officers. *Conference (1st : Manchester)*

See the 'Labour Party' example in rule 24.13 Type 5. Compare this form of a conference heading with that shown in frames 138 and 148.

Proceed to frame 142

FRAME 160

The answers that you should have are:

Church of England. *Diocese of York*

and

Catholic Church. *Archdiocese of Washington*

Rules 24.27C2 and 24.27C3 apply.

This completes our study of 'forms of heading'.

Proceed to phase 5, following frame 161.

FRAME 161

The answer is that entry is to be made directly under name in accordance with rule 24.1, ie:

British Goat Society

United States Capitol Historical Society

These are not government bodies, so that entries such as

Great Britain. *Goat Society*

and

United States. *Capitol Historical Society*

94

or

Washington. *United States Capitol Historical Society*
would be completely wrong. The first incorrect entry, in any case,
distorts the name and this pitfall should be avoided.

Proceed to frame 134

UNIFORM TITLES

AACR 2 Chapter 25

Major examples of works with varying titles are:

1) Sacred scriptures, eg the *Bible*, which is also known as the *Holy Bible* and by the names of its parts the *Old* and *New Testaments*.

2) Translations, eg Balzac's *Le père Goriot*, variously translated into English as *Goriot*, *Father Goriot* and *Old father Goriot*.

3) Music, eg Beethoven's *Piano sonata no 14*, otherwise known as the *Moonlight sonata*.

It is obviously helpful to choose one title as the single point at which all variations of the same work will be brought together in the catalogue.

A uniform title is, therefore, the particular title by which a work that has appeared under varying titles is to be identified for cataloguing purposes.

The relevant section of AACR 2 is Chapter 25 but it should be stressed that this is an *optional*, not an obligatory chapter.

The uniform title chosen is given before the title proper and is enclosed in square brackets, eg:

Carroll, Lewis
　[Alice in Wonderland]
　Alice's adventures in Wonderland.

When a uniform title is to be used and the work concerned would actually be entered under title according to the provisions of Chapter 21 of AACR 2, then the uniform title becomes the heading, eg:

[Arabian nights]

In this case the square brackets may optionally be omitted.

Read through rules 25.1 and 25.2 and then proceed to next frame

---

For works created after 1500, the title that has become best known through use or in reference sources should be chosen as the uniform title, eg:

Shakespeare, William
　[Hamlet]
　The tragicall historie of Hamlet . . .

However, the title of the original edition is used in doubtful cases or when no one title is established as being the one by which a work is best known.

Examine rule 25.3 and then choose a uniform title for the William Makepeace Thackeray novel *The history of Henry Esmond, Esq,*

Colonel in the service of Her Majesty Queen Anne, a work now familiarly known as *Henry Esmond*. Put your answer in the format used for uniform title layout as illustrated in the Shakespeare example given above.

Turn to frame 172 for the answer

FRAME 164

Rule 25.4 deals with works created before 1501 and directs that the title, in the original language, by which the work has become identified in modern reference sources, is to be preferred, eg:

[Nibelungenlied]
     Siegfried; translated from the middle high German.

If the evidence of modern reference sources is inconclusive, use the title most frequently found in either:

1   modern editions
2   early editions
3   manuscript copies

using the order of preference shown.

For classical Greek works, a well established English title is to be preferred when there is one, eg;

Aristotle
    [Ethics]
    Aristotelis ethica Nicolachea.

There is also provision in rule 25.4C for anonymous works created before 1501 and not written in Greek nor in the Roman script. Here the English title is to be used when there is one, eg:

[Book of the dead]

Read through rule 25.4 and then choose a uniform title for Aristotle's *De arte poetica liber*. In your answer use a layout similar to the other Aristotle example given above.

Turn to frame 176 for the answer

FRAME 165

Translations have the language of the translation added (rule 25.5D) after the uniform title, eg:

Verne, Jules

     [Vingt mille lieues sous les mers. English]

     Twenty thousand leagues under the sea.

    Formulate a similar uniform title entry for Nevil Shute's *Schach dem Schicksall*, the German version of *The chequer board*.

    Turn to frame 171 for the answer

FRAME 166

Rule 25.6 deals with uniform titles for parts of a work. Read through this rule. Note that if an item consists of three or more non-consecutive or unnumbered parts of, or extracts from, a work, then the uniform title for the whole work is used followed by 'Selections', eg:

[Arabian nights. Selections]

     Tales from the Arabian nights

The use of 'Selections' as a *collective* title is dealt with in rule 25.9.

    For an item which consists of, or purports to consist of, the complete works of a person, the collective title 'Works' is used (see rule 25.8), eg:

Shakespeare, William

     [Works]

     Complete works

    Read through the rules for collective titles (rule 25.8 to 25.12) and then choose a uniform title for a further Shakespearean work entitled *Complete plays*. Use a layout similar to that of the other Shakespeare example above.

    Turn to frame 175 for the answer

FRAME 167

Special rules in Chapter 25 deal with composite manuscripts, incunabula, legal materials, sacred scriptures, liturgical works and music. These rules, 25.13 to 25.36, should be examined by the student but it is not the intention of this program to cover them in detail. One or two examples will suffice to illustrate AACR 2's approach to such items.

                                                 (*continued*)

Legal materials are covered by rules 25.15 (Laws) and 25.16 (Treaties). The uniform titles 'Laws, etc' and 'Treaties, etc' respectively are used for collections of these items, eg:

United States
    [Laws, etc.]
    United States code . . .

For a single legislative enactment, the uniform title is chosen using the following order of preference:
1)   official short title or citation title
2)   an unofficial short title or citation title used in legal literature
3)   the official title of the enactment
4)   any other official designation.

An example of (1) would be:

United Kingdom
    [Education Act (1944)]

Read through rules 25.15 and 25.16 and then decide upon a uniform title for an *Agreement between the governments of the United States and Canada* dated 31 July, 1977.

Turn to frame 173 for the answer.

FRAME 168

Where sacred scriptures are concerned, the uniform title to be used is the title by which a sacred scripture is most commonly identified in English language reference sources dealing with the religious group to which the scripture belongs. If no such sources are available, general reference sources may be used. Headings such as:

    Avesta . . .
    Koran . . .

are therefore obtained.

The uniform title 'Bible' is used for the *Bible* and any of its parts. Added to this heading are the designation of the part, when this is necessary; the language of the text; the name of the version, or an alternative such as the translator or reviser; and the year of publication, eg:

    Bible. *N.T. English. Amplified. 1968*

Additions to the uniform titles for other sacred scriptures are made in accordance with the rule relating to the specific scripture: 25.18B– Talmud; 25.18K–Avesta; and so on.

Examine rules 25.17 and 25.18 and then choose a uniform title for *Selections, in English, from the Jewish sacred scriptures.*

Turn to frame 170 for the answer

FRAME 169

When formulating uniform titles for musical works, the general rules 25.1 to 25.7 may be used insofar as they are applicable and unless contradicted by the more specific rules 25.26 to 25.36, eg:

Porter, Cole
[Night and day . . .]
Nat og dag . . .

Where the work has a title consisting solely of the name of a type of composition, generally the accepted English form of name should be used, in the plural unless the composer wrote only one work of the type, eg:

Geminiani, Francesco
[Sonatas . . .]
Sonate . . .

To the uniform title must be added, where appropriate and where the title consists solely of a type, the medium of performance (rule 25.29) and any other identifying elements (rule 25.31), such as serial number, opus number and key, eg:

Beethoven, Ludwig van
[Sonatas, piano, no.14, op. 27, no. 2, C# minor]
Moonlight sonata

Examine rules 25.25 to 25.36 and then answer the following questions:

a) What would be the uniform title selected for a German version of a vocal score of *The Messiah*, which is entitled *Der Messias*?

b) What would be the uniform title selected for an arrangement of *Clair de lune*, which is from Debussy's *Suite bergamasque*?

Turn to frame 174 for the answers

FRAME 170

The answer is (see rule 25.18B):
Talmud. *English. Selections*
Proceed to frame 169

FRAME 171

The uniform title that would be chosen in this instance is the original English title, *The chequer board*. The language of the translation is German and this would be indicated after the uniform title. The answer is, therefore:

Shute, Nevil
[The chequer board. German]
Schach dem Schicksall.

It is immediately apparent how useful this type of uniform title entry can be.

Proceed to frame 166

FRAME 172

The later title, *Henry Esmond,* is the better known and this should be chosen as the uniform title. The answer is, therefore:

Thackeray, William Makepeace
[Henry Esmond]
The history of Henry Esmond, Esq. Colonel in the service of Her Majesty Queen Anne.

If you were right proceed to frame 164. If wrong, re-examine rule 25.3A before proceeding.

FRAME 173

The answer (see rule 25.16B1) is:

United States
[Treaties, etc. Canada, 1977 Jul. 31]

or

Canada
[Treaties, etc. United States, 1977 Jul. 31]

Proceed to frame 168

FRAME 174

The title to be used as a uniform title for a musical work is the composer's original title in the language in which it was formulated (rule 25.27A). If the item being catalogued is a 'vocal score', this is added to the uniform title (rule 25.31B3). If the text of a vocal work is a translation, the name of the language is also added (rule 25.31B7).

The answer to (a), therefore, is:

[Messiah. Vocal score. German]

The Messiah is actually used as an example in rules 25.31B3 and 25.31B7 of AACR 2, so that you should have had little difficulty in answering this question.

The title of the whole work is used as a uniform title for a separately published part; this is followed by a title of the part (rule 25.32A1). For an arrangement entered under the original composer, 'arr.' is added to the uniform title preceded by a semi-colon (rule 25.31B2). The answer to (b), therefore, is:

[Suite bergamasque. Clair de lune; arr.]

This completes our study of uniform titles. Proceed to phase six, following frame 176.

FRAME 175
The answer, provided by rule 25.10, is:

Shakespeare, William
[Plays]
Complete plays

Proceed to frame 167

FRAME 176
It should have been reasonably easy to discover that the 'well established English title' is *Poetics* and the answer is, therefore:

Aristotle
[Poetics]
De arte poetica liber.

Proceed to frame 165

PHASE SIX

REFERENCES

AACR 2 Requirements summarised in Chapter 26

Rules in the preceding chapters of Part II of AACR 2 indicate particular types of references that are made in specific circumstances.

FRAME 177

Having decided upon the form that headings chosen as access points will take, in accordance with the rules in Chapters 22 to 25, alternative forms of these headings must be considered.

The basic rule (26.1) states that: 'Whenever the name of a person or corporate body or the title of a work is, or may reasonably be, known under a form that is not the one used as a name heading or uniform title, refer from that form to the one that has been used'.

For example, as Jeanne Bourgeois is to be entered under her pseudonym Mistinguett (see frame 105 and 128), a reference is required from the form not used:

Bourgeois, Jeanne
    see **Mistinguett**

Similarly, for the corporate heading Ladsirlac (see frames 135 and 157) a reference is needed:

Liverpool and District Scientific, Industrial and Research
Library Advisory Council
    see **Ladsirlac**

Formulate a reference from the alternative form of the heading:

Carr-Saunders, A.M

used in frame 121;

Turn to frame 193 for the answer

FRAME 178

In frames 177 and 193 we considered the 'see' reference. This is a 'signpost', which simply says to the catalogue user: 'You are going the wrong way, there is no information here, proceed via . . . where information *will* be found', eg:

United Nations. *World Health Organisation*
    see **World Health Organisation**

Formulate a 'see' reference for the United States Commission on Civil Rights (see frame 144).

Turn to frame 197 for the answer

FRAME 179

Another type of reference, the 'see also' reference, says to the catalogue user: 'Yes, there is some information here but you should also try . . . where further related information may be found', eg:

British Iron and Steel Research Association
see also **Iron and Steel Institute**

The above reference links two corporate headings which are related but which are entered independently. A similar reference may be made if the works of one person are made under two different headings, eg:

Amis, Kingsley
see also **Markham, Robert**

It should be obvious that, in these instances, a reference in the reverse direction will also be required, ie:

Iron and Steel Institute
see also **British Iron and Steel Research Association**

Markham, Robert
see also **Amis, Kingsley**

One of the difficulties with regard to the above 'see also' references is that the catalogue user is not being told *why* the two separate headings have been used for the body or person. This problem can be overcome by the use of the 'explanatory' reference, which provides more detailed guidance, eg:

Cooper, Dorothy
for works of this author written under pseudonyms,
see
Castillo, Carmen
Mason, Margaret
Newland, Jill
Saville, Shirley

Make a reverse reference from the first of the pseudonyms indicated above.

Turn to frame 191 for the answer

FRAME 180

The use of 'see', 'see also', and 'explanatory' references is explained in section 26.0; read through these introductory notes. Note that a 'see' or 'see also' reference may be made in the form of a 'name-title' reference when it is being made from a title which has been entered under a personal or corporate heading, eg:

> **Beethoven, Ludwig van**
>> Moonlight sonata
>>> *see* **Beethoven, Ludwig van**
>>>> Sonatas, piano, no.14, op27, no.2, C minor

> **Moonlight** sonata
>> *see* **Beethoven, Ludwig van**
>>> Sonatas, piano, no.14, op.27, no.2, C   minor

Proceed to next frame

FRAME 181

Where headings for persons are concerned, here are some illustrative examples of occasions when it will be necessary to make 'see' references:

a) Different names, eg real name and pseudonym:
> **Bell, Currer**
>> *see* **Bronte, Charlotte**

b) Different forms of name, eg:
> **Horatius Flaccus, Quintus**
>> *see* **Horace**

c) Different entry elements, eg:
> **Roche, Mazo de la**
>> *see* **De La Roche, Mazo**

The relevant rule, which should be examined, is 26.2A. Make a reference from the alternative form of the heading:

> **Bedford, Mary Russell,** *Duchess of*

Turn to frame 189 for the answer

FRAME 182

'See' references are made from alternative names of corporate bodies in instances such as:

a) Different names, eg:
> **Quakers**
>> *see* **Society of Friends**

b) Different forms of name, eg:
> **Roman Catholic Church**
>> *see* **Catholic Church**

111

c)   Different forms of heading, eg:

United States. *Tennessee Valley Authority*
   see **Tennessee Valley Authority**

The relevant rule is 26.3A. After examining this rule answer the following question.

If the filing system used in your catalogue files initials with full stops differently from those without full stops, is it necessary to refer from the form with full stops to a form without full stops, eg: from L.A.D.S.I.R.L.A.C. to Ladsirlac?

Turn to frame 196 for the answer

FRAME 183

'See also' references are dealt with in rule 26.2C for persons and rule 26.3B for corporate bodies. As explained in frame 179 they may be used to link the works of one person made under two different headings or to link two corporate bodies which are related but which are entered independently.

'See also' references are also made between related works which are entered under different uniform titles (see rule 26.4B1), eg:

Klage
   see also **Niebelungenlied**

and

Niebelungenlied
   see also **Klage**

Evan Hunter writes under both his real name and under his pseudonym, Ed McBain. How would you link these two names by means of 'see also' references?

Turn to frame 194 for the answer

FRAME 184

'See' and 'see also' references may be made in the form of 'name-title' references as explained in frame 180. Using the index to AACR 2, find the relevant rule for name-title references for names of persons. Turn to this rule and examine the examples contained therein. How is a name-title reference made from the inverted form of a heading which consists of initials?

Turn to frame 190 for the answer

FRAME 185

Certain explanatory references were considered in frame 179. The further examples given in rules 26.2D and 26.3C should also be studied.

Rule 26.2D deals with explanatory references for names of persons. Note the optional rule for prefixes (26.2D2).

Rule 26.3C covers explanatory references for corporate bodies. Typical instances where such references may be used are: to explain the scope of a heading; to link headings which supersede one another; to provide guidance in the way acronyms are filed.

The Liverpool Regional College of Technology was merged with the other Liverpool Colleges of Art, Building and Commerce to form the new Liverpool Polytechnic in 1970. Make an explanatory reference leading from the old to the new name.

Turn to frame 192 for the answer

FRAME 186

Care must be taken to ensure that appropriate references are made for entries involving uniform titles. Here is the first part of a main entry for the German version of Shute's *The chequer board* when a uniform title approach is used as shown in frame 171.

> **Shute, Nevil**
>> [The chequer board. German]
>> Schach dem Schicksall / Nevil Shute

This work would need an added title entry, ie:

> The **Chequer** board. German
>> Schach dem Schicksall / Nevil Shute

The following references would also be required:

> **Schach** dem Schicksall.
>> *see* **Shute**, Nevil
>>> [The chequer board. German]

> **Shute**, Nevil
>> Schach dem Schicksall
>> *see* **Shute**, Nevil
>>> [The chequer board. German]

Rule 26.4 deals with references for uniform titles.

Make appropriate references for the following item entered under uniform title, which was used as an example in frame 168.

> **Bible** *N.T. English. Amplified. 1968*
>> The amplified New Testament.

Turn to frame 188 for the answer

FRAME 187

References may be made in lieu of added entries if this leads to economy without inconvenience to the user of the catalogue. Examples of such references will be found in rule 26.5. After studying these examples, make an appropriate title reference for Charles Dickens *David Copperfield*, for use in the catalogue of a library which has many editions of this work.

Turn to frame 195 for the answer

FRAME 188

The references would be:

> The **Amplified** New Testament
> > *see* **Bible.** *N.T. English. Amplified. 1968*

> **New Testament**
> > *see* **Bible.** *N.T.*

> **Holy Bible**
> > *see* **Bible**

The latter two references would obviously serve for all New Testaments and/or Bibles.

If you were not correct read through rules 26.4A1 and 26.4A3 very carefully.

If you were correct, you should still make a careful note of the various examples included in these rules.

Proceed to frame 187

FRAME 189

The answer is:

> **Russell, Mary,** *Duchess of Bedford*
> > *see* **Bedford, Mary Russell,** *Duchess of*

The reference is made from family name to the better known title of nobility in accordance with rule 26.2A1. The example for the duchesse d'Abrantès in rule 22.6A should also be studied.

Proceed to frame 182

FRAME 190

It should have been quite easy to find the relevant rule, 26.2B, by consulting 'Name-title references—personal names' in the index.

Name-title references from the inverted form of initials are covered by rule 26.2B2, the format being:

D., H.
    Helidora and other poems
      see **H.D.**

Proceed to frame 185

FRAME 191

The answer is:

Castillo, Carmen
    For works of this author written under her real name,
see
Cooper, Dorothy
    For works written under her other pseudonyms, see
Mason, Margaret
Newland, Jill
Saville, Shirley

If you were incorrect examine the Lauran Paine example included in rule 26.2D1.

Proceed to frame 180

FRAME 192

The answer is:

Liverpool Regional College of Technology
    The Liverpool Regional College of Technology merged with the other Liverpool Colleges of Art, Building and Commerce in 1970 to form the Liverpool Polytechnic. Works by these bodies are entered under the name used at the time of publication.

If you were incorrect, re-examine the examples under *Change of name* in rule 26.3C1.

Proceed to frame 186

FRAME 193

It is possible that a catalogue user might search for A.M. Carr-Saunders under the name Saunders. As Carr-Saunders has been chosen as the form of heading, a reference must be made from the other form. The answer is, therefore:

> **Saunders, A.M. Carr-**
> > *see* **Carr-Saunders, A.M.**

Proceed to frame 178

FRAME 194

The names would be linked by 'see also' references in either direction, ie:

> **Hunter, Evan**
> > *see also* **McBain, Ed**
>
> **McBain, Ed**
> > *see also* **Hunter, Evan**

If you were incorrect, look at frame 179 and rule 26.2C again before proceeding to frame 184

FRAME 195

The reference should read:

> David Copperfield
>
> **Dickens, Charles**
> > Editions of this work will be found under **Dickens, Charles**

This version conforms to rule 26.5A. The alternative method shown in rule 26.5B should also be noted.

This completes our study of references.

Proceed to phase seven, following frame 197.

FRAME 196

Yes, a reference would be required as shown in rule 26.3A4, ie:

> **L.A.D.S.I.R.L.A.C.**
> > *see* **Ladsirlac**

Remember that a further reference would be required from the full form of the name (see frame 177).

Proceed to frame 183

FRAME 197

The answer is:

Commission on Civil Rights
see **United States.** *Commission on Civil Rights*

This is an example of a reference from an alternative form of heading when entry has been made as a subheading under the name of a higher body. Compare with the example for the World Health Organisation in frame 178.

Proceed to frame 179

ANALYSIS

AACR 2 Chapter 13

Chapter 13 is, of course, in Part I of AACR 2. It was thought advisable to defer a study of this special aspect of description until this later stage of the program

FRAME 198

Analysis is the process of preparing a bibliographic record which describes a *part* or *parts* of a larger entity.

A 'part' might be a separate item which is contained in a monographic series or in a multipart monograph; A 'part' might also be 'physically' subsumed within a more comprehensive work, eg: the text of a single play within a collection of plays; an article in a serial; one musical composition from a sound recording containing a number of compositions; etc.

Analysis might, indeed, be concerned with any 'part' of an item, even down to a single, significant paragraph, or an illustration, if these were considered important enough to be so treated.

It is obviously impossible, therefore, to legislate as to what will or will not be done, with regard to analysis, by a particular cataloguing agency. Analysis may be achieved in various ways and, in addition, the *degree* to which analysis can be undertaken may be limited by finance, staff, or some other constraint. Each agency must determine its own individual policy. Because of this, Chapter 13 simply lays down general guidelines to assist in the selection of methods of analysis.

Proceed to next frame

FRAME 199

In general, there are four main ways in which analysis may be achieved:

1) A complete bibliographic description may be prepared for the part (rule 13.2), eg:

English history, 1914-1945 / A.J.P. Taylor. — Oxford : Clarendon Press, 1965. — xxvii, 709 p., [1] folded leaf of plates : ill., maps ; 23 cm. — (The Oxford history of England ; v.15). — Bibliography: p.602-639.

Here, the item is part of a monographic series and the title of the part is not dependent upon that of the comprehensive item. The details of the comprehensive item are given in the series area.

2) A 'contents' note may be made in a detailed entry for the larger work (rule 13.3), eg:*

Contents: The noblest monument of English prose / by John Livingston Lowes — The English Bible / by W. Macneile Dixon — The English Bible / by A. Clutton-Brock — On reading the Bible / by Arthur Quiller Couch.

* *See also example of contents note in frame 21*

This technique is the simplest means of analysis and the bibliographic description of the part is usually limited to a citation of the title or a statement of responsibility and a title.

3)　　An analytical *added* entry may be made for the part (rule 13.4), eg:

The moving toyshop : a detective story / by Edmund Crispin. — p.210-450 ; 30 cm.
In The Gollancz detective omnibus. — London : Gollancz, 1951

The loved one / by Evelyn Waugh. — p.78-159 ; 17 cm.
In Horizon. — Vol.17, no.98 (Feb. 1948)

This method is linked with (2) in that, if a 'part' has already been cited in a comprehensive entry for the work as a whole, an added analytical entry, providing direct access to the part, may also be made.

The two examples show the basic formats for analytical entries for a part of a monograph and a part of a serial. Note that the citation for the whole item begins with the word '*In*' (italicised, underlined, or otherwise emphasised) and basically consists of the main entry heading; the title proper; the publication details (of a monographic item), or the numeric designation (of a serial). This citation is known as an 'In' analytic note.

4)　　Multi-level description may be used (rule 13.6), eg:

American folklore / co-ordinated for the Voice of America by Tristram Coffin. — Washington : United States Information Agency [production company]. — sound tape reels ; 7½ ips, mono. ; 7 in. — (Forum series).
8: The American traditional ballad / G.M. Laws. — 1967. — 1 sound tape reel (35 min.). — Includes illustrative excerpts.

Here, the description is divided into two or more levels. The first level records information relating to the item as a whole. The second and, if necessary, subsequent levels record information relating to the part or parts. The levels are made distinct by layout or typography.

It becomes obvious that some of these methods are related to provisions found elsewhere in AACR 2 but, for convenience, the various methods of analysis are also collected together and described in this one chapter.

Proceed to next frame

Read through rules 13.1 to 13.5, carefully examining the further
examples of analysis included therein.

On pages 132 to 146 of W A Munford's *Penny rate: aspects of British
public library history, 1850-1950* appears a section by Joan Edmondson
entitled *Mechanics' institutes and public libraries. Penny rate* was published in London by The Library Association in 1951 and is 22 cm. high.
a)   Formulate a 'contents' note for the section which would appear
     in a comprehensive entry for the item as a whole.
b)   Produce an analytical added entry for the section.
Turn to frame 202 for the answers

After examining rule 13.6 and its illustrative examples, attempt to
produce a multi-level description for the following item:

METHODS IN CELL BIOLOGY

Edited by David M. Prescott

Volume 11

YEAST CELLS

1975

This multipart work is published in New York and London by Academic
Press. The particular volume has 12 pages numbered in Roman and 332
pages numbered in Arabic; it is illustrated and is 24 centimetres in
height. Its ISBN is 0-12-564111-7
Turn to frame 203 for the answer

The contents note would appear as follows:
     Includes: Mechanics' institutes and public libraries / Joan
  Edmondson: p.132-146
See rule 2.7B18.

The analytical entry would be:

Mechanics' institutes and public libraries / Joan Edmondson. — p.132-146 ; 22 cm.
In Munford, W.A. Penny rate : aspects of British public library history. — London : Library Association, 1951

If you were incorrect, re-examine frame 199 and rule 13.4 before proceeding to frame 201

FRAME 203
The multi-level description would be:

Methods in cell biology / edited by David M. Prescott. — New York ; London : Academic Press.
Vol. 11: Yeast cells. — 1975. — xii, 332 p. : ill. ; 24 cm. — ISBN 0-12-564111-7.

This answer is formulated in accordance with rule 13.6 but note how the general rules for description from Chapter 1 are also relevant to a certain extent. It should be noted that London could be omitted from the publication area if this item was being catalogued by an agency outside the U.K.
This completes our study of 'Analysis'. Proceed to phase eight.

PHASE EIGHT

WORKED EXAMPLES

FRAME 204

You should now be able to catalogue an item fully (apart from classification and subject work) using all of the sections and rules of AACR 2.
The frames in this phase are designed to test whether you can, in fact,
do this.

First of all, you are required to produce a full description for the
following book, ie a printed monograph; add to your description a main
entry heading to make a complete catalogue entry and indicate the headings under which you would make added entries. Note the numbers of
the AACR 2 rules that you use.

The title page of the book contains the information:

CHESS TACTICS

PUZZLES FOR
BEGINNERS

R.G. WADE
RAYMOND BOTT
STANLEY MORRISON

LUTTERWORTH PRESS
GUILDFORD AND LONDON

On the verso of the title page appears 'Revised edition 1973'. Opposite
the title page appears 'Lutterworth Chess Series 3'. The book contains
95 pages numbered in Arabic and it consists mainly of illustrations. It
is twenty centimetres high and its ISBN is 0-1788-1658-7.

Turn to frame 212 for the answer

FRAME 205

Reproduced overleaf is a map of Merseyside. Produce a full description
for this map. What would you choose as the main entry heading?

Turn to frame 214 for the answer

merseyside

after local government
reorganisation in 1974

Lancashire

Southport

Greater Manchester

Wigan

Formby

Ormskirk

Skelmersdale

SEFTON
AREA Sq.MILES 56.6
POP. 307,200

Maghull

Rainford

Billinge

Ashton-in-Makerfield

Crosby
Litherland

Kirkby

Haydock

Bootle

St. HELENS
AREA Sq.MILES 51.5
POP. 193,500

Newton-le-Willows

KNOWSLEY
37.6
POP. 191,700

Wallasey

LIVERPOOL
AREA Sq.MILES 43.4
POP. 561,100

Prescot

Hoylake

Whiston

Huyton

Warrington

Birkenhead

WIRRAL
AREA Sq.MILES 60.3
POP. 349,200

Widnes

Bebington

Heswall

Hale

Eastham

Runcorn

Neston

Cheshire

▬▬▬▬ County Boundary

———— District Boundary

Scale Six miles to one inch
Published by
Merseyside County Council Public Relations Office
1975

33-1/3 RPM

Made in England Ⓟ 1973

SIDE 1

'ALL TIME
CLASSICS'

A D E C1

Stereo

London Symphony

Orchestra

Conducted by

Ezra Rachlin

OVERTURE—FANTASY: 'ROMEO AND JULIET'—
Peter Ilytich Tchaikovsky
OVERTURE: 'THE MARRIAGE OF FIGARO'—
Wolfgang Amadeus Mozart
SABRE DANCE—*Aram Khatchaturian*

TEACHING GEOGRAPHY

Volume 3 Number 4

Subscription enquiries: Longman Group Ltd, Journals Division, 43/45 Annandale Street, Edinburgh EH7 4AT, Scotland. **Published** for the Geographical Association by Longman Group Ltd, Journals Division, Longman House, Burnt Mill, Harlow, Essex CM20 2JE, Telephone 0279 26721, to whom all advertising enquiries should be directed. Volume 4 will be published in 4 issues: July [1978], November [1978], January [1979], April [1979].
Annual subscription £5.00 USA $12.00 Single numbers £1.50 USA $4.00

Geographical Association

April 1978

FORTHCOMING ISSUES:

The Belvoir Coalfield: where to sink the mine? [David Symes & Derek Spooner]; **developing a field centre for one's own school** [J. R. Doughty & A. Hancock]; **fieldwork exchanges save money** [John Rawlings]; **using GYSL throughout the school** [Judith Mansell]; **spending one's departmental allocation: a case of priorities** [Bruce Weston]; **using a landscape evaluation technique** [Leslie Ellison].

April 1978   **Editor:** *Patrick Bailey*

ISSN 0305-8018

WORLDS

MEMBER LIBRARIES
1 Putnam County District Library
2 Brumback Library
3 Lima Public Library
4 Lima State Hospital
5 Ada Public Library
6 Hardin County District Library
7 Rockford-Carnegie Library
8 Dwyer-Mercer County District Library
9 Coldwater Public Library
10 Fort Recovery Public Library
11 St. Marys Community Public Library
12 Auglaize County Public Library
13 Amos Memorial Public Library
14 Logan County District Library

ASSOCIATE LIBRARIES
15 Wright State University-Western Ohio
Branch Campus Library
16 Lima Memorial Hospital-Health
Sciences Library

WESTERN
OHIO
REGIONAL
LIBRARY
DEVELOPMENT
SYSTEM

PUTNAM
1

VAN WERT
2

ALLEN
4
3 16

5 HARDIN
6

MERCER
7
8 15 11
9
10

AUGLAIZE
12

LOGAN
14

SHELBY
13

131

FRAME 206

Given on page 129 is the information which appears on the label of one side of a sound disc which is twelve inches in diameter. The label on the other side is similar except for the side number and the list of musical works recorded on that side. The playing time of the record is not stated but, from the size of the playing area and the playing speed, it can be assumed to be about sixty minutes. The address of Arcade Records is not given on the item but it is known to be London. Produce a full catalogue entry (complete with main entry heading but *omitting* a contents note) for the recording. What added entries would be required?

Turn to frame 213 for the answer

FRAME 207

One of the problems involved in the cataloguing of serials is that, usually, the cataloguer has to try to describe an *incomplete* item. Very often reference sources have to be consulted to ascertain when a serial first began publication, etc. Assume that your library began to subscribe to the serial *Teaching geography* with issue number four of volume 3, some details of which are shown on page 130. A check reveals that this serial began publication with the April 1975 issue and that four or five issues a year are published. The serial is illustrated and its height is 30 centimetres. Produce a full description for this item. What would be the heading for the main entry?

Turn to frame 211 for the answer

FRAME 208

It is, of course, possible to catalogue any sort of item using AACR 2. To illustrate this, let us assume that it is considered necessary to catalogue a book-bag which is intended as an advertisement for the regional library system WORLDS. The information which is given on the bag is shown on page 131; it is given in red lettering on a white background. The bag measures 43 x 33 cm. Produce a catalogue entry for this item complete with main entry heading. What other entries would be required for the item? Although no date appears on the item, it is known to have been issued in the 1970s.

Turn to frame 215 for the answer

FRAME 209

With regard to the answers to the problems in this phase, it should be noted that AACR 2 provides for a particular library or cataloguing agency to make an individual decision in certain instances, eg:

1) A 'general material designation' is an *optional* inclusion following the title proper (see frame 14), eg:
   Chess tactics [text] : puzzles for beginners
   Merseyside after local government reorganisation in 1974 [map] *
   All time classics [sound recording]
2) Paragraphing could replace punctuation (. –) for the separation of areas in the description (see frame 5).
3) AACR 2 prescribes three levels of detail in the description according to the requirements of individual libraries (see frame 23);
4) In certain cases an abbreviated designation of function may be added to an added entry heading for a person, eg: *ed.* ; *comp.* , etc. (see rule 21.OD).

There may well be other differences in individual methods, eg capital or lower case letters in headings:

COLLEGE OF WILLIAM AND MARY

or

College of William and Mary

Each cataloguing agency will need to develop its own 'in-house' layout.

Whatever practices are followed in a particular library, however, they should be followed *consistently*, lack of consistency leads to a chaotic catalogue.

Proceed to frame 216

FRAME 210

The added analytical entry would be:

Sabre dance / Aram Khatchaturian. – on side 1 of 1 sound disc (ca. 2½ min.) : 33 1/3 rpm, stereo. ; 12 in.

In London Symphony Orchestra. All time classics. – London : Arcade, 1973

Check this entry against your answer, referring, if necessary, to the examples included in rule 13.5A.

* *North American usage. British usage would give [cartographic material] See rule 1.1C1*

Note that if author analytical entries were required, then a decision would have to be made as to the manner in which the name was to be entered. It appears, for instance, spelled in different ways on various musical works, eg Khachaturian. The latter is the more usual form of spelling and if an entry was made under that, ie

> **Khachaturian, Aram**
>> Sabre dance . . .

then a reference would have to be made from the alternative form:

> **Khatchaturian, Aram**
>> *see* **Khachaturian, Aram**

Remember that references must always be made from variant forms of heading under which a person or body might be known.

Make sure that you understand the points made in this and the previous frame (213) before proceeding to frame 207

FRAME 211
The description would be:

> Teaching geography. – Vol.1, no.1 (Apr. 1973)- . – Harlow : Longman Group for the Geographical Association, 1973- . – v. : ill. ; 30 cm. – 4 or 5 issues yearly. – Library has: v.3, no.4 (Apr. 1978)- . – ISSN 0305-8018.

Some of the relevant rules used for this entry were:

Volume designation and dating	12.3
Words or phrases indicating function of publisher	1.4D3
Physical description	12.5
ISSN	1.8B and 12.8B
Frequency note	12.7B1
Holdings note	1.7B20 and 12.7B20

Check your answer against the above entry, referring when necessary to the rules noted.

The main entry would be under title, ie the first words of the description, according to rule 21.1C.

Proceed to frame 208

FRAME 212

The complete catalogue entry, the *main entry*, would be:

Wade, R.G
    Chess tactics : puzzles for beginners / R.G. Wade, Raymond
Bott, Stanley Morrison. — Rev. ed. — Guildford : Lutterworth,
1973. — 95 p. : chiefly ill. ; 20 cm. — (Lutterworth chess series ;
3). — ISBN 0-1788-1658-7.

Added entries would be necessary for the other contributors:
    Bott, Raymond
    Morrison, Stanley
for the title:
    Chess tactics : puzzles for beginners
and for the series:
    Lutterworth chess series
    Among the rules used were the following:
Description

title and statement of responsibility	1.1 and 2.1
title proper	1.1B and 2.1B
sub-title, ie other title information	1.1E1 and 2.1E1
statement of resonsibility	1.1F and 2.1F
edition statement	1.2 and 2.2
abbreviations	Appendix B
publication details	1.4
only one place named	1.4B8
physical description	1.5 and 2.5
work consisting mainly of illus-trations	2.5C6
series statement	1.6 and 2.6
numbering	1.6G
ISBN	1.8 and 2.8
Choice of main entry heading	21.6C1
added entry under each of other contributors	21.6C1 and 21.30B
added entry under title	21.30J
added entry under series	21.30L
Instruction relating to the way in which headings for persons are to be entered	21.1A, 22.1B, 22.4A and 22.4B3

    If your entries were correct—proceed to frame 205.

If they were not correct, examine the entries produced above and check them against the rules indicated. Proceed only when you are certain that you understand the way in which the entries have been formulated.

FRAME 213
The complete catalogue entry for the sound recording would be:

> **London Symphony Orchestra**
> All time classics / London Symphony Orchestra ; conducted by Ezra Rachlin. — [London] : Arcade, 1973. — 1 sound disc (ca. 60 min.) : 33 1/3 rpm, stereo. ; 12 in. — ADE C1.

This is a reasonably straightforward item to catalogue. Points to note are:

i)   The place of publication is given in square brackets (see rule 1.4A2).
ii) The conductor could, alternatively, be named in a note rather than in the statement of responsibility area (see rules 6.1F and 6.7B6).
iii) Although you were not asked for a contents note, rule 6.7B18 instructs that one should be given, ie:

> Contents : Romeo and Juliet : overture (Fantasy) / Peter Ilytich Tchaikovsky — The marriage of Figaro : overture / Wolfgang Amadeus Mozart — Sabre dance / Aram Khatchaturian

and the other items from the other side of the record would be included.

The main entry heading is chosen in accordance with rule 21.23C: 'enter a sound recording containing works by different persons under the person or body represented as principal performer'. The body is entered directly under its name as directed in rule 24.1.

An added entry would be required for the title:
> All time classics

but an added entry would not be required for the conductor of the orchestra *unless* this was considered to be an important access point by the particular cataloguing agency.

Assuming that a contents note had been made as shown in (iii) above, produce an added analytical entry for the *Sabre dance*, which lasts for about two and a half minutes.

Turn to frame 210 for the answer

FRAME 214

The full description for the map would be:

> Merseyside after local government reorganisation in 1974. –
> Scale 1 : 380,160. – Merseyside : Merseyside County Council,
> Public Relations Office, 1975. – 1 map ; 16 x 12 cm.

The rules in Chapter 3 ('Cartographic materials') of AACR 2 for the recording of the title and publication details refer back to the relevant rules in Chapter 1, ie 1.1, 1.1B and 1.4. The scale is recorded as a ratio as indicated in rule 3.3B.* Note that, optionally, scale information as given on the map may be added. The physical description is recorded as instructed in 3.5. Check your answer against the above entry, referring as necessary to the appropriate rules.

As there is no indication of 'responsibility' on the item, it would be treated as a work of unknown authorship and main entry would, therefore, be under title, ie the first words of the description (rule 21.5).

Added entries are not really necessary unless it is considered that the heading for the Public Relations Office of Merseyside County Council would provide an 'important access point' (see rule 21.30F). This is a decision for the individual cataloguing agency. If an added entry was made, the heading would take the form:

Merseyside. *Public Relations Office*

Rules 24.18 and 24.19 should be examined to see how this heading has been formulated.

Proceed to frame 206

FRAME 215

The main entry would be:

WORLDS

> WORLDS : Western Ohio Regional Library Development
> System. – [Ohio : WORLDS, 197-]. – 1 book-bag : plastic, red
> and white ; 43 x 33 cm.

The cataloguing of this item would be covered by Chapter 1 and Chapter 10 (three dimensional artefacts). The title is taken from the

---

* *The scale is given on the map as 'six miles to one inch'. This means that one mile is represented by one sixth of an inch. To convert this to a ratio, calculate how many 'sixths of an inch' are in one mile. 6 miles = one inch; therefore 1 mile = 1/6 inch; therefore ratio is 1 : 6 x 63360 (where 63360 is the number of inches in a mile), = 1 : 380,160*

item itself and recorded in accordance with rule 1.1B. The name of a publisher or distributor is not given on the item but it is obviously distributed by WORLDS. The name of the state can be given as the place of 'publication' (see rule 1.4C6). The date is recorded as 'sometime in the 1970s'. All of the publication area must be enclosed in square brackets as it does not appear in the chief source of information, ie the item itself. The physical description details have been recorded in accordance with the following rules:

specific name of item	10.5B1
material	10.5C1
colours named if in one or two colours	10.5C2
dimensions	10.5D

The bag is intended as an advertisement for WORLDS; it depicts a sketch map of the area covered by WORLDS and lists the libraries which are members. It can therefore be said to deal with the corporate body itself and main entry is under the heading for that body according to 21.1B2a;

The brief form of name is the one that predominates on the item and, in any case, the brief form would take precedence over the full form as the chosen form of heading (rule 24.2D).

No title added entry would be required as the title proper is the same as the main entry heading (rule 21.30J1):

References would be required; one from the full form of name (rule 26.3A):

Western Ohio Regional Library Development System
see **WORLDS**

and, in libraries which file initials with full stops differently from those without full stops (rule 26.3A4):

W.O.R.L.D.S.
see **WORLDS**

Proceed to frame 209

FRAME 216

FINAL NOTE

This completes your study of the basic principles of AACR 2. If you have worked through this program assiduously, you should now have a sound basis of knowledge from which to progress, so that, with more practice, you should be able to make very good use of what is arguably the best code of cataloguing rules ever produced. It may, however, be necessary to return to this program and revise certain sections. To facilitate this, most of the frames with informational content are, as you may have noticed, arranged consecutively within each phase so that they can be read in sequence simply by omitting to answer the set questions. The index will assist in the location of frames dealing with specific problems.

INDEX

Unless otherwise stated, numbers refer to frames. When a topic is dealt with in a sequence of frames, only the first relevant number is usually given.

142

147